Jacobs v. Alvarez

Case File

Trial Materials

Jacobs v. Alvarez

Case File

Trial Materials

Taylor Rex Robertson
Vice President—Global Litigation and Employment
Co-Chair and Chief Case Architect, Texas High School Mock Trial Competition
Certified Sommelier, WSET Level 3, US Open Blind Tasting Champion—2019
Dallas, Texas

NITA®
National Institute for Trial Advocacy

Address inquiries to:
Reprint Permission
National Institute for Trial Advocacy
325 W. South Boulder Rd., Ste. 1
Louisville, CO 80027–1130
Phone: (800) 225-6482
Email: publications@nita.org

ISBN 979-8-88669-085-9
FBA 2085
eISBN 979-8-88669-086-6
eFBA 2086

Printed in the United States of America

ASPEN PUBLISHING

Official co-publisher of NITA.
aspenpublishing.com/NITA

TABLE OF CONTENTS

SELECT LAW, JURY INSTRUCTIONS, AND VERDICT FORM

APPENDICES

Acknowledgments

The author would like to thank the following people for their invaluable assistance in the creation of this case file:

Jessica Amyett
Robert Manley
Honorable Josh Burgess
Scott Fredericks
Aimee M. Furness
Joe Pinto
Chase Imgrund
Shannon Mercer
Jacob Fergus

CASE SUMMARY

Fact Pattern

Jordan Jacobs and Payton Alvarez are partners in the Wine Imports and Distribution Partnership. Recently, Jacobs and Alvarez voluntarily dissolved the partnership by mutual agreement. Near the end of the dissolution process, Jacobs and Alvarez signed a settlement agreement that governed the resolution of two final matters: 1) negotiating termination of two long-term purchase contracts with two French winemakers; and 2) selling the partnership's rare wine collection at auction.

In December YR-1, Jacobs flew to France for eight days and ultimately negotiated a mutual termination of both contracts for $41,500. At the same time, Alvarez analyzed proposals from two auction houses and ultimately chose to sell the wine collection with a private auction house called Coveted Collections. Coveted Collections organized an auction with several high-net-worth individuals on short notice and sold the wine before Jacobs's return. The net proceeds from the auction were approximately $135,000.

Upon returning from France and learning of the auction, Jacobs filed a lawsuit against Alvarez for breach of contract and alleged that Alvarez failed to liquidate the wine collection "in the best interest of an orderly dissolution," as required by the settlement agreement and Nita law. Specifically, Jacobs alleged the private auction was hasty, too expensive, failed to generate sufficient proceeds, and was inferior to a public auction proposal Alvarez received from Allen Virtual Auction House.

Alvarez denies that the private auction was not in the best interest of an orderly dissolution and asserts two affirmative defenses: that Jacobs either 1) consented to Alvarez's decision in advance; or 2) ratified Alvarez's decision after it occurred. The case is now set for a jury trial to resolve the claims. This is a bifurcated trial on the issue of liability only; if the jury finds Alvarez liable, there will be a separate trial at a future date to determine the amount (if any) of damages.

The partnership agreement is included in the case file as Exhibit 1, and the settlement agreement is Exhibit 2. The applicable law is contained in the select provisions of the Nita Uniform Partnership Code and the jury instructions, both of which appear near the end of the case file.

Cast of Characters:

Jordan Jacobs:	Plaintiff; partner of partnership; former banking executive
Payton Alvarez:	Defendant; partner of partnership; former sommelier
Riley Allen:	Owner of Allen Virtual Auction House ("AVAH")
Kondo Mineaux:	Managing director of Coveted Collections
Courtney "Corky" Gardner:	Wine investor; attended auction at Coveted Collections
Parker Roberts:	Wine expert, including valuations and auctions

Frederic Veronique:	Owner of Domaine Veronique et fils, a winery in Burgundy
Jerome Rolande:	Owner of Chateau Rolande, a winery in Burgundy
Del Murphy:	Appraisal expert employed by AVAH; recently deceased
Alex Lang:	Employee at partnership's bank

Instructions for Use

When this case file is used for a bench or jury trial, the following witnesses may be called:

For Plaintiff:

Jordan Jacobs

Riley Allen

For Defendant:

Payton Alvarez

Kondo Mineaux

Corky Garner is an optional additional witness. The instructor will decide whether participants may only use the deposition or if Corky may be called to the stand for direct or cross.

All years in these materials are stated in the following form:

- YR-0 indicates the actual year in which the case is being tried (i.e., the present year);
- YR-1 indicates the next preceding year (please use the actual year);
- YR-2 indicates the second preceding year (please use the actual year); etc.

Case facts and references to the Designated Sommelier's Exam and the US and French World Wine Tasting Match competitions are fictionalized versions of real-life events, simplified for use in this case file. Please do not rely on outside knowledge or experience when reading the fact patterns and exhibits.

Suggested Time Limits for Full Trial

Voir Dire	10 minutes per side
Opening Statement	10 minutes per side
Witness Examinations	60 minutes per side
Closing Argument	10 minutes per side

Electronic copies of the exhibits can be found at the following website:

http://bit.ly/1P20Jea
Password: Jacobs1

Court Filings

IN THE SUPERIOR COURT
IN AND FOR THE COUNTY OF DARROW
AND STATE OF NITA

JORDAN JACOBS	§	
Plaintiff,	§	
	§	
v.	§	Civil Action No. 95-1984
	§	
PAYTON ALVAREZ	§	
Defendant.	§	

PLAINTIFF'S ORIGINAL COMPLAINT

Plaintiff Jordan Jacobs ("Jacobs") files this Original Complaint against Defendant Payton Alvarez ("Alvarez") for breach of contract and states as follows:

Background Facts

1. Jacobs and Alvarez created the Wine Imports and Distribution Partnership ("the partnership"), effective January 1, YR-10, after winning the World Wine Tasting Championship. Jacobs, a former banking executive, focused on the partnership's import business—selecting and purchasing wines for the business portfolio, and coordinating the importation process of the same wine. Alvarez, a former sommelier, focused on the distribution side of the partnership—selling and delivering the partnership's wine portfolio to retailers, restaurants, bars, and package stores.

2. While the partnership was an immense success, Jacobs and Alvarez mutually agreed in August YR-1 that it was time to move on. They instituted a voluntary dissolution of the partnership without court supervision.

3. On November 1, YR-1, Jacobs and Alvarez executed a settlement agreement in which they agreed the dissolution process to date was proper and each accepted responsibility to resolve one of two remaining dissolution matters. Jacobs was responsible for negotiating the termination of two long-term purchase contracts, and Alvarez was responsible for determining how to liquidate the partnership's rare wine collection. The settlement agreement provided that Jacobs could file an action if Alvarez selected an auction that was not "in the best interest of an orderly dissolution" as defined in the Nita UPC.

Cause of Action

4. The settlement agreement is a valid, enforceable contract. All of Jacobs's obligations and conditions precedent to seeking relief under the settlement agreement have been fully performed, satisfied, or waived. Alvarez breached the settlement agreement by choosing to sell the wine collection by private auction with Coveted Collections, which was plainly

not in the best interest of an orderly dissolution. Jacobs has been damaged in an amount to be determined at trial.

5. Jacobs hereby demands a trial by jury in this cause of action.

DATED: December 15, YR-1

Respectfully submitted,

WALTON & ASSOCIATES

By: *Olivia W. Walton*

Olivia W. Walton
Attorney for Plaintiff Jordan Jacobs
Nita Bar No. 24144
444 Main Street, Suite 202
Nita City, Nita 99991
(819) 555-3030

IN THE SUPERIOR COURT
IN AND FOR THE COUNTY OF DARROW
AND STATE OF NITA

JORDAN JACOBS Plaintiff,	§ § §	
v.	§	Civil Action No. 95-1984
PAYTON ALVAREZ Defendant.	§ § §	

DEFENDANT'S ORIGINAL ANSWER AND AFFIRMATIVE DEFENSES

Defendant Payton Alvarez ("Alvarez") files this Original Answer and Affirmative Defenses to Plaintiff Jordan Jacobs's ("Jacobs") Original Complaint and respectfully states as follows:

Factual Background

1. Alvarez admits the allegations in Paragraphs 1–2. Alvarez admits the allegations in the first two sentences of Paragraph 3. The settlement agreement speaks for itself; otherwise, to the extent a further response to Paragraph 3 is required, denied.

Cause of Action

2. Alvarez admits the allegations in the first sentence of Paragraph 4. Alvarez denies the allegations in the rest of Paragraph 4. Alvarez demands and agrees to a jury trial in this case.

Affirmative Defenses

3. The following affirmative defenses, in whole or in part, bar Jacobs's recovery on their breach of contract claim: (1) consent; and/or (2) ratification.

DATED: December 29, YR-1

Respectfully submitted,

BRUDER LAW

By: *Andrew P. Bruder*

Andrew P. Bruder
Attorney for Defendant Payton Alvarez
Nita Bar No. 18455
2323 Central Avenue, 12th Floor
Nita City, Nita 99991
(819) 555-8855

IN THE SUPERIOR COURT
IN AND FOR THE COUNTY OF DARROW
AND STATE OF NITA

JORDAN JACOBS Plaintiff,	§ § §	
v.	§	Civil Action No. 95-1984
PAYTON ALVAREZ Defendant.	§ § § §	

STIPULATIONS

The parties agree and stipulate to the following:

1. This is a civil trial that will be tried before a jury. This is a bifurcated trial on the issue of liability only. Should Alvarez be found liable, a separate trial will be held at a later date to determine the amount (if any) of damages.
2. At all relevant times, the time in France (including Burgundy) is seven hours ahead of the time in Nita.
3. Unless expressly noted otherwise, all dates and times in the pleadings, depositions, and exhibits are the dates and times in Nita.
4. The settlement agreement is a valid, enforceable contract and no party, witness, or attorney may dispute or raise any objection to any part of the dissolution process that occurred prior to the execution of the settlement agreement.
5. All prices or dollar figures in the case materials are in US dollars.
6. The court's charge, verdict forms, and jury instructions are accurate and complete in all respects, and no objections to them will be entertained.
7. All exhibits included in the case materials are authentic and are accurate copies of the originals. No objections to the authenticity of the exhibits will be entertained. The only exhibits to be used at trial are those included in the case packet.
8. All the witness depositions were written and signed on the dates indicated in each deposition. The signatures on the witness depositions and on all other documents are authentic. None of the witnesses read any of the other depositions prior to writing their own. Any comment about the claims of other witnesses are based either on speculation or on conversations and/or personal observations that the witnesses held prior to the filing of the suit.
9. The court has both subject matter and personal jurisdiction over the parties. All questions of fact will be submitted to a jury. Questions of law will be decided by the court.

10. Exhibit 16 is selected information about the wines sold at auction during December YR-1 that are relevant to this case. The information in Exhibit 16 is derived from Parker Roberts's subscription website, which is considered the most accurate and detailed price estimate website for rare bottles of wine in the United States.

11. Two of the wines sold by Coveted Collections on December 7, YR-1, have been consumed and one, the 1955 Champagne, has been resold. The partnership has no right to demand return of the wines sold at that auction, and no purchaser has agreed to do so.

12. Burgundian wine law provides that individuals with an ownership interest in a dissolved, terminated, or non existent entity bear personal liability for any claims a French citizen may have against the entity.

13. Exhibits 3, 4, 15, 16, and 20 are business records as defined by Rule 803(6) of the Federal Rules of Evidence.

14. Exhibit 6 is the document named "AVAH RFP Response to WIND Partnership.pdf" attached to the email in Exhibit 5.

15. Exhibit 8 is the document named "Coveted Collection RFP Response (SIGNED).pdf" attached to the email in Exhibit 7. The unsigned version of this document was attached to the email in Exhibit 17.

16. Kondo Mineaux sent Exhibit 9 to Payton Alvarez by email on December 8, YR-1, at 10:14 p.m.

17. Exhibits 12, 13, and 14 were the attachments to Jordan Jacobs's email in Exhibit 11.

18. Courtney "Corky" Gardner may be out of the country and the State of Nita on the date of trial and, if so, may be treated as an unavailable witness under Rule 804 of the Federal Rules of Evidence.

19. The checks in Exhibit 12 and 13 have been cashed but not yet accounted for in the cash balance of the partnership.

DATED: Day of Trial.

Respectfully submitted,

WALTON & ASSOCIATES

By: *Olivia W. Walton*

Olivia W. Walton
Attorney for Plaintiff
Nita Bar No. 24144
444 Main Street, Suite 202
Nita City, Nita 99991
(819) 555-3030

BRUDER LAW

By: *Andrew P. Bruder*

Andrew P. Bruder
Attorney for Defendant
Nita Bar No. 18455
2323 Central Avenue, 12th Floor
Nita City, Nita 99991
(819) 555-8855

Depositions

IN THE SUPERIOR COURT
IN AND FOR THE COUNTY OF DARROW
AND STATE OF NITA

JORDAN JACOBS Plaintiff,	§ § §	
v.	§ §	Civil Action No. 95-1984
PAYTON ALVAREZ Defendant.	§ §	

DEPOSITION OF JORDAN JACOBS

I, Jordan Jacobs, hereby swear the following statements are true and correct to the best of my knowledge:

I am forty-four years old and a partner of the Wine Imports and Distribution Partnership with a 50 percent ownership interest. Payton Alvarez is the only other partner in the partnership, and Payton also owns a 50 percent interest in the partnership.

I live in Nita with my spouse, Brit, but we have plans to travel the globe as soon as this case is over. We have two children, twins, who are twenty and currently juniors at Northwestern.

After nine years, Payton and I mutually decided to dissolve the partnership and started the voluntary dissolution process set out in our partnership agreement, which is Exhibit 1. In September YR-1, we were almost finished with the dissolution process—selling all our assets for cash and settling all our debts and liabilities. To expedite the end of dissolution, Payton and I executed a settlement agreement that gave us each responsibility to resolve one of the two remaining items in the dissolution. Once those were resolved and accounted for in the cash balance, we would then split the cash equally. Our settlement agreement is Exhibit 2.

The settlement agreement imposed certain requirements and obligations on Payton and me when resolving the two remaining items. Payton failed to follow those requirements and obligations when deciding to sell the partnership's rare wine collection at a hasty private auction with Coveted Collections. Those wines have already been resold—and, in a few instances, consumed—so I have no choice but to file a lawsuit to hold Payton accountable for the damages caused by that decision.

History with Payton Alvarez

I have known Payton for more than ten years, and I still consider Payton a friend to this day. I met Payton when we were both studying for the difficult Designated Sommelier's Exam, back in March YR-11. We first met at Carved, a steakhouse where Payton was working. Payton noticed

I was studying for the Level 3 DSE exam—the same that Payton was preparing for. To become a designated somm, as they are known around the industry, you must pass four levels of exams—and you can only attempt an exam once per year, so it's a minimum of four years from start to finish. No one has ever earned a DSE pin in less than eight years. In fact, less than one percent of those who attempt the Level 1 DSE exam ultimately make it through all four exams. It's brutal.

In YR-11, I was working as vice president of construction loans at Nita State Bank. The job was okay and paid very well, but banking was losing its luster for me. I think that's why I started looking into the DSE exam; just something to do other than banking. I had always been interested in wine production and wine history, and I guess I was able to channel my studying discipline from getting my MBA because I absolutely crushed the first two DSE exams, level one and level two.

But the level three exam was an exponential increase in difficulty. There is a written theory exam covering literally any fact or history related to wine, a mock service exam as if you were a sommelier at a fancy restaurant, and the most dreaded thirty-minute oral exam in history—the blind wine tasting exam. These three parts make up the level 3 exam, and you have to pass each part, or you fail the whole thing. You could get a perfect theory and mock service score but fall just one point shy of the cut-off to pass blind tasting, and you would fail the whole thing.

Maybe I should have become an engineer because I cannot handle not being able to figure something out. So, I studied and practiced for months to improve my blind tasting skills. Sure, that involves drinking wine, but you are always spitting when you are blind tasting to avoid frying your palate. There are six wines, three white and three red, that are presented pre-poured in glasses for the thirty-minute tasting exam. You get points for correctly identifying certain aspects of the wine, such as the main grape varietal, the country and region where it was grown, the year the grapes were harvested, and for identifying the correct level of certain wine components like acidity or tannin.

We both failed the level 3 exam in May YR-11 because of the blind tasting component. After, Payton and I agreed to focus exclusively on blind tasting. At first, we started meeting three or four times a week to blind taste wines the other had brought. We then expanded into a larger group of blind tasters so we could experience more wines at each study session. At some point, Payton and I learned about this blind tasting competition in California that sends the winner to France to compete against other countries on behalf of the United States. The most interesting part of the competition was that it was a pairs competition. This meant each team had two people tasting the same wines but submitting one collective answer. Payton and I had tasted so much together that we were keenly aware of each other's strengths and weaknesses. For example, Payton rarely missed identifying a Tempranillo from Rioja, Spain—so if Payton said it was Rioja and I wasn't confident it was something else, I knew I could trust Payton's call.

Our teamwork was unstoppable. We finished the California competition with 112 points, and the next closest team barely managed to clear 70. That was in July YR-11. We studied for another month and then headed to France.

And our luck continued in earnest at the world competition in August YR-11. There were thirty-nine other countries there—some fascinating people to meet—but most of them didn't think too highly of the two Americans. We soon changed their minds. Payton and I felt pretty good about our answers at the end of the world competition, and all we wanted was to finish in the top half of the competitors. So, we were utterly shocked when they announced the USA as the champion of the world wine tasting match. We won! We couldn't believe it. Things were absolutely wild after that. We appeared on a dozen morning shows, were interviewed by several major news reporters, and appeared in articles from all over the world—including one by Parker Roberts. I have a copy of it somewhere that I can provide. I can barely remember it all.

But I do specifically remember during all the wackiness, I think mid-December YR-11, that I proposed to Payton that we set up our own company. Payton had been working as a sommelier for several years and knew a lot of folks in the Nita food and beverage industry. I had traveled to Europe throughout my entire life and had a plethora of experience examining new businesses and their financing. Ultimately, we settled on an importation and distribution business focused specifically on sourcing wines from outside the United States. There were already too many distributors in Nita sourcing American wine, mostly from California, so we decided to attack the market with international wines. France, Spain, Italy—you know.

The Wine and Distribution Partnership

On December 30, YR-11, Payton and I signed a partnership agreement for the partnership and electronically filed the necessary documents to register the partnership for business under Nita law the next day. The partnership agreement itself became effective on January 1, YR-10.

I handled the importation side of the business. I traveled to Europe, visited wineries and vineyards, selected the wines we wanted in our portfolio, and then handled the logistics to get the wine to Nita and through customs.

Payton handled the distribution part of the business, meeting with wine retailers (wine bars, restaurants, package stores) and selling them wines from our portfolio. Payton also managed the delivery of the wine to each establishment and generally served as the account manager for each of our customers. Once the wines cleared customs, they were delivered to our Nita warehouse for storage until they were sold and delivered to one of our customers. I can't deny that Payton handled the distribution side of our partnership masterfully. We were a perfect pair, as tasting partners and business partners.

About seven years into the partnership, though, Payton started pressing me to consider wines from other countries with emerging winery businesses—Egypt, China, Mexico. Payton complained that European wines weren't exotic enough. I resisted this idea—first of all, we were already importing high-quality wines from small vineyards, wines you can't buy in your local supermarket. And I have a relationship with those vintners. I didn't want to be chasing all over China, trying to find quality wines in a country where I can't even read the road signs.

It became increasingly clear that Payton and I no longer shared the same vision for the business. So, after a nine-year run, we mutually agreed that it was time to close the partnership and move on. I personally was done with working and looked forward to traveling to Europe for pleasure rather than for business. Payton is about ten years younger than I—not quite ready to retire—and wanted to start a new business focused on introducing wines from new countries to Nita. I believe Payton's plan was to contract with a variety of importers, rather than create a new partnership (our portfolio ceased once the partnership ended), but you'd have to ask Payton about that for more details.

In September YR-1, we officially started to dissolve the partnership. Payton and I came up with a plan to sell all the partnership's assets, resolve all outstanding debts and liabilities, and then split the remaining proceeds. Exactly what the partnership agreement provided. Much like our day-to-day division of labor, I handled everything related to the importation side—terminating contracts with the European wine growers, closing accounts, and all the administrative details. Payton handled everything on the distribution side, including selling off the remaining inventory of wine and terminating the lease for our warehouse.

Everything went extremely well during the dissolution process—until the last two remaining issues: first, selling the partnership's collection of rare wine—eight coveted bottles of wine that we had purchased as investments during our early years and stored in pristine condition in our warehouse—and second, terminating two purchase contracts with French winemakers.

The Hasty and Surreptitious Wine Sale

To expedite the resolution of the two remaining items, and to ensure we agreed on everything that had happened to date, Payton and I executed the settlement agreement. I was responsible for negotiating a mutual termination with two of our French wine suppliers. We had a purchase contract with each of them that obligated the partnership to continue buying wine for two more years, which we obviously weren't going to do since we were dissolving the partnership. Burgundian law is peculiar—claims against a dissolved company can be made against the individual owners. If the partnership didn't purchase the wine from these winemakers (which it wouldn't since it was being dissolved), those winemakers could technically sue Payton and me personally sometime in the future. So, my job was to fly to France and negotiate a settlement with both winemakers to get us out of those contracts. Payton and I agreed on a total budget of $75,000 for the settlement payments, travel costs, and reasonable expenses. I was set to depart on December 2, YR-1.

While it was Payton's job to decide how to sell the wine collection, Payton was obligated to make sure whatever auction was picked was in the best interest of an orderly liquidation. Before I left for Europe, Payton was still very unsure what to do, asking me all sorts of questions, reading and re-reading all the proposals from auction houses. I'm not saying it was an easy task for Payton, but neither was mine—and Payton was earning money for the partnership; I was trying to make sure we paid out as little as possible. I recall telling Payton that we could discuss the auction choices by email while I was traveling and away. I distinctly remember not agreeing or consenting to any auction type at that time.

We essentially had two options—a public auction or a private auction. I was strongly in support of a public auction because it had the greatest potential to generate the highest proceeds. The more people there to bid, the higher the bid will naturally go, right? I recall that Payton favored a private auction at the time—during a call we had on December 1, which I remember because I was packing—but, again, Payton was still unsure. I think Payton preferred that option because a private auction could be completed faster than a public auction, but I don't remember Payton having that strong of feelings about it. I expected us to pick up the discussion when I returned to the States.

But when I returned on December 10, Payton had already sold the wine by private auction—while I was out of the country! Payton met me at the airport when I landed, which I thought a bit odd; it had never happened before. Once we were in the car, Payton asked me to confirm all the travel expenses charged to the partnership credit card—which I did. Payton typed a bunch of things on the phone and then said everything was concluded with the partnership—and that we should head to the bank to split the money. Payton said I could send the travel itinerary and receipts next week or "if ever" because Payton trusted me. Of course I provided them—they are Exhibit 14.

I was a little jetlagged, so it took a second for these statements to register with me. I asked about the wine collection, and Payton said it had all been sold and the funds were in our bank account. I asked how that was possible. Payton said Coveted Collections threw together a private auction in downtown Nita. I asked how much we made—just over $135,000. That was it?! I remember seeing the Coveted Collections estimates at one point in Exhibit 8 while I was in Europe—I still thought they were just in a proposal phase at the time—and the estimates for half of the bottles totaled more than that, I think.

I refused to go to the bank and said I was displeased Payton held the auction without telling me—and seemingly had taken steps to keep me in the dark. Payton told me not to worry and to see the value of everything being done. We could move on, and I could finally retire, Payton said.

Sure, but we only had about a half million in cash after everything else had been liquidated and sold. My estimates and the things I read said our wine collection should've sold for $200,000, maybe $250,000. The worst was when I learned that Payton never even tried to negotiate the fees with Coveted Collections—despite specifically agreeing to do so!

The more I thought about it, the angrier I got. Payton wants to get on with this new distribution business. I get all that, but not at the expense of getting pennies on the dollar from a business we built together. I may soon be retired, but you need money to keep traveling—and I intend to do so, sparing no expense.

Payton is probably my best friend, but I have to protect my rights as a partner in the partnership before the cash is accounted and divvied up. I have that right specifically in the settlement agreement. Payton should never have sold the wine at private auction because it generated far less money than any estimate or appraisal, was not in the best interest of an orderly dissolution, and was done, basically, in secret. To me, that shows Payton was trying to pull a fast one—and knew it. Heck, even the famous Parker Roberts all but commanded Payton to shop around and negotiate the fees for an auction of our wine. Just look at Exhibit 15. I know for a fact that Payton reads everything Parker Roberts puts out, almost like it's automatic.

No Consent—No Ratification

Payton alleges that I somehow consented or ratified the terrible decision to sell our wine collection with Coveted Collections. False on both accounts. I never consented to using Coveted Collections before the auction took place. I had barely read the proposal by the time Payton signed with Coveted Collections—without my consent and while I was in France, by the way. I also received absolutely no update from Payton when I repeatedly asked about the auction house decision, further showing that Payton was trying to do it all in secret.

As for me somehow consenting to or ratifying the decision after the auction took place, there's no evidence of that, either. Sure, I responded to Payton's email in Exhibit 11 asking for the receipts and information from the France trip, but I certainly did not say anything forgiving Payton for that terrible decision. I don't even mention Coveted Collections in my email and I don't remember seeing the final invoice attached to Payton's. I'm simply giving Payton evidence of my expenses as a good partner and friend so there is no question about the money I spent on behalf of the partnership. I was also horribly jetlagged and shocked by Payton's antics when I landed in Nita. I was in no condition to ratify anything, even if I did—which I did not.

I also have seen the snippet of text messages between Payton and me in Exhibit 10. I barely remember that exchange because I was literally getting on the plane in Nita headed for France. But regardless, I certainly didn't consent or ratify or bless anything there regarding Coveted Collections hosting the auction for our rare wine. The only thing I agreed to in Exhibit 10 is that Payton should follow the settlement agreement.

I do remember Payton asking me repeatedly to go to our bank to authorize them to split the proceeds, and maybe I said "yes" at one point during the car ride from the airport to get Payton off my back. But I never intended to go, nor did I go. The next day, I was already meeting with my lawyers for this case.

I declare under penalty of perjury that the foregoing is true and accurate to the best of my knowledge.

Jordan Jacobs

Dated: January 2, YR-0

Signed and sworn before me on January 2, YR-0

Casey Stamos

Notary Public

IN THE SUPERIOR COURT
IN AND FOR THE COUNTY OF DARROW
AND STATE OF NITA

JORDAN JACOBS Plaintiff,	§ § §	
v.	§	Civil Action No. 95-1984
PAYTON ALVAREZ Defendant.	§ § § §	

DEPOSITION OF PAYTON ALVAREZ

I, Payton Alvarez, hereby swear the following statements are true and correct to the best of my knowledge:

I am thirty-four years old, and I have known Jordan for the last twelve years. I am single but I have been dating Remy Houston for the past five years and living together the last two in downtown Nita. We do not have any children nor plan to anytime soon.

Our partnership, the Wine Imports and Distribution Partnership, or WIND—pronounced like it rhymes with "wine"—was a great success. But we both agreed it was time to move on. The voluntary dissolution process was running smoothly, and we executed a settlement agreement to address the two small remaining issues in dissolution.

I still consider Jordan a great friend, but I am ready to move on with my next business venture—Alvarez Distributions. I am still shocked that Jordan took so much issue with the private sale of our wine collection at Coveted Collections. Yes, the auction did not raise as much money as the high side of some of the estimates, but that's all part of auction. With all due respect to Jordan, I believe that Jordan is playing Captain Hindsight with all of this.

Let me be clear: my decision to sell the partnership's wine at a private auction hosted by Coveted Collections was in the best interest of an orderly dissolution. No auction would have been perfect, yet that seems to be what Jordan is complaining about. What a shame.

My History with Jordan Jacobs

Before Jordan and I won the US and World tasting competitions in mid-YR-11, I was working as an assistant sommelier on the floor at a local restaurant named Carved. It's a steakhouse with a thick wine menu and an enormous wine cellar in the basement right under the sprawling dining room. During a weekend dinner rush, Carved might see 250 covers—heads, or people, in restaurant speak—so you can imagine the chaos.

I met Jordan while working at Carved, in fact. To make some extra money, I frequently picked up lunch shifts at Carved. They are easier shifts than the dinner rush but still with decent potential to make a little money. One Saturday afternoon, I was working behind the bar and Jordan sat down to have lunch. After a little while, I noticed that Jordan was studying materials for the Designated Sommelier's Exam (the "DSE"). As it turned out, Jordan and I were studying for the level 3 exam later that May. I was a bit shocked Jordan had passed the level 2 exam, being a banking executive of some sort. But, as time when on, I totally understood why Jordan had passed—Jordan was wicked smart.

After that, we studied together, three or more times a week, leading up to the big exam date. Sadly, even though we passed the other two portions, we both failed the blind tasting portion of the level 3 exam that year, so we failed the overall exam. I was disappointed and a little downtrodden, if I'm being honest. But not Jordan. Jordan was already planning how we could get better at our blind tasting skills. More than just tasting together or in small groups. "We need competition reps," Jordan said on many occasions.

That led us to the US blind tasting competition in July YR-11—which we won without much of a sweat—and then to the World Wine Tasting Match in the Loire Valley a month later. After we had submitted our scores and were waiting for the results, I remember telling Jordan that I hadn't felt that good about a blind tasting in a long time. I felt like we had done well. Together, we had promised to try and make it into the top half of the bracket. There were thirty-nine other countries competing that year, and we just wanted to be twentieth or better. I am pretty sure I screamed when they said the United States was the overall winner. They only read the top ten names before publishing the final rankings, so we weren't expecting to hear, "the United States," period. But sure enough, we had prevailed. It was crazy after that. TV shows and newspaper articles.

The Partnership and Dissolution

At some point, we decided that we were great partners and should try our hands at the business side. We discussed the idea over the holidays and signed a partnership agreement effective January 1, YR-10. That is Exhibit 1.

During the partnership, I managed the distribution side of the business while Jordan imported the wine. Jordan purchased wine from winemakers in France, Italy, and sometimes Spain, and then managed all the logistics of getting the wine to Nita. Once the wine cleared customs in Nita, I managed the sale and delivery of the wine to our customers—restaurants, wine bars, retailers, and package stores.

It was a great success and invigorating while we got our feet on the ground. I learned that I loved seeking out new clients, educating them about the exclusive vineyards we represented, and winning contracts. I had a whole system for assuring restaurants that they wouldn't see the exact same wine list at another restaurant, that they had wines no one could buy at a retailer. I earned their trust and got the whole system running like a well-oiled machine. But once I had everything running so well, I found myself getting bored. Where was the challenge? I got to thinking about other regions, places that were just developing their vineyards and wineries. Like China. Parts of China are at the same latitudes as California vineyards; it made perfect sense for them to plant vineyards. Sure enough, China's wine production is going gangbusters. Articles about China led me to other surprising wine regions. Egypt, for one. I ignored South America—it's already been played, no challenge there. I'm talking to growers in Vietnam now, encouraging them to up their production, think about exporting. It's all exciting, and I love being in on the ground floor.

Unfortunately, Jordan doesn't share my enthusiasm for this new adventure. It led to a lot of friction when I encouraged trips to China or Mexico—Jordan loves spending time in Italy and France more than the business side, honestly. That's just who Jordan is. Jumping from banking to the partnership was the one big risk my friend ever took. Don't get me wrong; I'll always be grateful that Jordan took the leap with me, but all things must come to an end. On August 18, YR-1, Jordan and I agreed to a voluntary dissolution of the partnership. We worked together to liquidate the assets and settle the partnership's debts. Under the partnership agreement, once we had liquidated and settled everything, Jordan and I would split the remaining cash 50/50.

To try and advance the process, we executed a settlement agreement that gave us each responsibility over one of the issues to manage toward resolution. You can see that in Exhibit 2. I quickly prepared a request for proposal (RFP) to send to local auction houses. I asked for details of how they would organize an auction for our specific wine collection, the type of people who would be bidding, the types of fees and costs we would incur, the time to the auction and collection, all that stuff. The RFP that I sent to the auction houses on November 20, YR-1, is my email contained in Exhibits 5, 7, and 17.

Coveted Collections

I also researched the pros and cons of selling the wine collection by public or private auction. Kondo Mineaux and Riley Allen both called to get the list of wines we wanted to sell, Riley on November 20 and Kondo on November 22. Jordan and I had agreed that those were the only worthy auction houses in Nita. Both auction houses came by on November 27 to physically inspect the wines as well.

I received a response to the RFP from both of those auction houses, and you can see those in Exhibits 5 and 7. Those were sent to me as attachments, which are Exhibits 6 and 8, respectively.

After reviewing that information, I called Jordan and explained why I believed a private auction with Coveted Collections was the best option. That was November 30, YR-1, a few days after both auction houses inspected our wine collection. You see, the settlement agreement required that the auction be in the best interest of an orderly dissolution. And I was in charge of liquidating the wine collection.

Jordan asked a bunch of questions and seemed to favor the public auction option, but agreed on a private auction when I explained it would be a faster process. After all, it was the last thing we needed to do to close the dissolution. Well, that's not entirely true, I guess. Jordan still had to close two accounts in France. We had contracts to purchase wine from them next year, which we obviously weren't going to do after we dissolved the partnership, so Jordan had to go over there to sign some settlement documents with those winemakers. French law required signatures in person, evidently—and Jordan still needed to negotiate a settlement payment amount that would get those winemakers to agree to mutually terminate those contracts.

So, Jordan went off to France on December 2, YR-1, to negotiate those documents, and I organized the private sale. On December 3, I signed the proposal from Coveted Collections, a preeminent private auction house that specializes in selling rare wine. You can see my signature on Exhibit 8, which I sent back to Coveted Collections that same day, as noted in Exhibit 7. They had a select client list and assured me they could get a sizeable—and wealthy—group together on fairly short notice. Because two of their most favorable bidders were going on a trip to Antarctica soon, we set the auction to happen in a few days. The auction was set for December 7, and I intended to go but had a minor family emergency that I had to tend to that day.

From what I heard and read, it was a good turnout—twelve bidders each with a net worth of over a million dollars, and all with a desire for rare wine. Sure, I was a little disappointed that the two Bordeaux bottles did not go for more, and those sale prices were quite a bit below the auction house's estimates, but we still netted more than $130,000 after everything was said and done. The entire process also took less than a week. You can see the information about how the auction went in the documents Coveted Collection sent me, including Exhibit 9.

Sure, I'm an avid reader and fan of Parker Roberts, probably the most famous expert in wine and wine sales anywhere in the world. I read all Parker's articles and columns, so of course I've seen what is in Exhibit 15 and the article about Jordan and I winning the World Competition that's Exhibit 20. And, yes, I probably saw Exhibit 15 a day or two after it was posted, but that article is vague and more entertainment than expertise. I read it, but it did not have any effect on my decision for the auction of our rare wine collection. I've also routinely reviewed Parker Roberts's wine valuations because I have a diamond subscription to the Vine Acuity website and content. I certainly checked the estimates I received against Parker's estimate ranges, but those are hardly guarantees. In any event, both auction houses were reasonably within Parker's estimates, so I had no concerns with Coveted Collections or AVAH.

I never did anything to try and hide the private auction from Jordan. I don't think Jordan is lying, but I think Jordan is misremembering. At any rate, there's no guarantee the wine would have sold for more if we used a public auction—but there is a guarantee that it would have taken longer. Much longer. Best interest of an orderly dissolution? The private auction checks all those boxes.

Jordan Consented and Ratified My Decision

Jordan also agreed to the private auction in at least two ways. First, Jordan consented before we had the auction in our text message exchange in Exhibit 10. Jordan also ratified the decision after the fact as you can see in our email exchange in Exhibit 11. I was taken aback when Jordan threw a fit when they got back to Nita and learned about the private auction. I sent Jordan the proposal from Coveted Collections in Exhibit 17, so obviously I wasn't trying to hide anything, but I don't think there was any need for how Jordan responded.

Jordan also agreed with me on December 10 during the drive back from the airport that we would go to the bank the next morning to authorize the cash proceeds to be split. I even called the bank and set up a meeting with our bank representative, Alex Lang, the next day on December 11. But Jordan no-showed.

Finally, I want to clarify my next business venture—Alvarez Distributions. My business plan is to purchase wines from importers and essentially continue my distribution empire in Nita. I have established some great roots and connections over the past nine years, and I am eager—antsy, in fact—to get past this lawsuit and start my own company.

I declare under penalty of perjury that the foregoing is true and accurate to the best of my knowledge.

Payton Alvarez

Dated: January 8, YR-0

Signed and sworn before me on January 8, YR-0

Casey Stamos

Notary Public

**IN THE SUPERIOR COURT
IN AND FOR THE COUNTY OF DARROW
AND STATE OF NITA**

JORDAN JACOBS Plaintiff,	§	
	§	
v.	§	Civil Action No. 95-1984
	§	
PAYTON ALVAREZ Defendant.	§	
	§	

DEPOSITION OF RILEY ALLEN

I, Riley Allen, hereby swear the following statements are true and correct to the best of my knowledge:

I am Riley Allen, forty-eight years old, and the managing director of Allen Virtual Auction House ("AVAH"). AVAH is an online public auction house that was inspired by my parents many years ago in YR-24. My mom was an avid antique shopper, and my father just loved the internet and online marketplaces. Eventually, they created a website to sell some of the antiques my mom had collected over the years, and that became a huge success. They were eventually bought out by one of those big online resellers you've heard about, and they used that money to create a much more sophisticated marketplace—now known as AVAH.

I currently live in north Nita in the ranch-style house that I inherited from my parents (along with AVAH) when they both passed away in YR-8. I am single and live alone.

AVAH started with items that were consigned of any value, but now it focuses exclusively on items valued at $1,000 or more. AVAH has been around for about ten years now, and in that time, we've hosted three rare wine auctions, all in December YR-1. Wine isn't the most popular category of items we sell, but it's gaining in popularity based on the number of users and bids we've seen in those three wine auctions.

I received a request for proposal ("RFP") from Payton Alvarez on behalf of the WIND Partnership on November 20, YR-1, which you can see in Exhibit 5. I called Payton and got the wine list immediately, and then AVAH promptly started work analyzing the wines, considering how to market the auction, and numerous other factors. We at AVAH had been wanting to get into the investment-grade wine auction space, and we had done a lot of homework to make sure it fit with our business model. When I got the RFP from Payton, I was stoked that this was the perfect opportunity for us to enter the wine auction market. We attended the inspection day with our in-house appraiser on November 27, YR-1. AVAH had recently hired our appraiser, Del Murphy, as part of our transformation into auctioning wine. Del did some amazing analysis and work that helped us prepare our proposal in Exhibit 6. Unfortunately, Del got really sick over the holidays and passed away suddenly. It was terrible. Del was an amazing figure in the wine analytics world. Del's memo to me after the appraisal is Exhibit 19, for what it's worth. I did rely on Del's notes to prepare the proposal I sent back to Payton and the partnership.

After we analyzed and reviewed all the data and information, I responded back to Payton with our proposal (Exhibit 6) by email on November 30 (Exhibit 5). I never heard back, even though we were essentially ready to go as soon as the proposal contract was signed—but it never was. Sure, it would have taken a little time to prepare the wine for marketing, announce the online auction, and then commit to it. I followed up with Payton once or twice by phone but never received a response or call back from Payton.

On December 8, I was shocked to learn that the partnership's rare wine collection was sold at a private auction, let alone at Coveted Collections. There were only twelve bidders present? That is pretty low, if you ask me. No wonder the wines didn't sell for what AVAH had estimated. And, from what I know now, the sale was also well short of Coveted Collections' estimate. Check out Exhibit 8—big whiff, right?

How do I know what happened at the Coveted Collection auction if I wasn't there? Well, I personally know someone who attended—Courtney Gardner. "Corky" is a long-time investor in, and aficionado of, rare and valuable wine, and Corky has been at nearly every wine auction held in the past three or four years, from what I hear. In any event, the day after the auction, Corky called me about auctioning off a wine they'd purchased at a Coveted Collection auction. I met Corky to look at the wine, and I was stunned—it was a 1955 bottle of Champagne. The same one I had inspected a couple weeks earlier with Payton and Del. Corky said they won the bottle for $18,000. I about fell over. That bottle is worth $25K minimum!

We ultimately sold that bottle in our first public wine auction on December 17, YR-1, where we sold off four bottles for more than $75,000. You can see the results and details of that auction and two others we held in December YR-1 in Exhibit 18. The 1955 Champagne was the star of the show—selling for $27,600. That right there is proof that the Coveted Collection auction was suspicious at best. Sure, it was great for Corky (and later us too!), but hardly in the best interest of the person or entity selling the wine.

As an expert in auctions myself, I also have to criticize Coveted Collections for the order the wines were put up on the auction block. You have to think about how much money is in the pot when choosing what items to auction off first, versus near the end, when you auction items off one by one. The Champagne is a perfect example—it went last in Coveted Collections' auction, when six figures had already been spent, and naturally went for a lower price than it should have. Why in the world did Coveted Collections list the Bordeaux first? And the Napa cab in the first three? It makes no sense to bury the highest value items near the end, at least for a private auction setting like this.

I am certain we would've raised more money for the partnership had we hosted the auction, but of course I cannot guarantee that outcome. But what I can guarantee as fact is that Coveted Collections' auction order was not in the best interest of the partnership, as evidenced by the fact the Champagne sold for significantly more just weeks later with AVAH. And Kondo Mineaux wants to claim we don't have real bidders? Our user base would have provided the partnership with a much larger universe of potential bidders. Just look at the increases in active users logged in over our last three wine auctions. Could all those users afford a $20,000 bottle of wine? Of course not, but what's to stop a few millionaires from logging on and buying wines at our auction? Nothing. Also, our fees are much lower than the private auction houses. We might pay our customers a little more slowly than Coveted Collections, but we guarantee payment in ten business days. That's not much of a difference to twenty-four hours in the grand scheme of things.

I have seen the article and evaluations by Parker Roberts in Exhibits 15 and 16. I absolutely revere Parker Roberts as the foremost expert in wine investments, wine auctions, and frankly anything related to wine. How Payton Alvarez could've read that article in Exhibit 15 and still thought a private auction was in the best interest of the partnership is inexplicable.

Finally, I should probably explain a little bit more about how the wine auctions at AVAH are formatted. We put one item up at a time, just like any other live auction, and users submit their bids. Every time someone makes a bid, the clock resets to ten seconds left. If the clock hits zero, the person with the last bid wins the item. Pretty simple really, much like a fantasy football draft auction, if you've ever played that. Does that mean some auctions last much longer than others? Of course, but that's all part of the fun. There's a very low risk that someone waiting for a later item would get bored or lose interest if the items ahead of them took too long to settle.

We also have a minimum floor bid that must be hit before we are obligated to sell the item. This is in our terms and conditions that every user agrees to. The minimum floor isn't revealed to the users for obvious reasons, but it's there for the seller's protection in case of an internet outage or other large event that might shut out all but a handful of bidders. In our three wine auctions to date, we've not had any issue surpassing the minimum floor. I've included those details in the summary of our recent auctions in Exhibit 18, which is a memo-to-file I created on January 1, YR-0. The total fees we collected from those three auctions was $31,000, and every seller was paid within ten business days—each on the eighth business day after the auction.

Of course, AVAH plans to hold additional wine auctions, but we are taking a small pause while this case plays out—just in case there are any takeaways from how AVAH can improve its marketing and customer retention.

I declare under penalty of perjury that the foregoing is true and accurate to the best of my knowledge.

Riley Allen

Dated: January 12, YR-0

Signed and sworn before me on January 12, YR-0

Casey Stamos

Notary Public

IN THE SUPERIOR COURT
IN AND FOR THE COUNTY OF DARROW
AND STATE OF NITA

JORDAN JACOBS Plaintiff, v. PAYTON ALVAREZ Defendant.	§ § § § § § § §	Civil Action No. 95-1984

DEPOSITION OF KONDO MINEAUX

I, Kondo Mineaux, hereby swear the following statements are true and correct to the best of my knowledge:

I am forty-seven years old. I was born and raised in Wimbledon, near London, in the UK, and moved to Nita in YR-19 to attend the Nita Business School. I live about twenty minutes north of downtown Nita with my spouse and our five dogs. All corgis—good enough for the late queen, good enough for us. I own Coveted Collections, a premier and exclusive private auction house that was founded right here in Nita nearly a century ago. That's right, Coveted Collections was founded in YR-94, and it's still here today. I purchased the company in YR-17 for $675,000 cash.

I am also the chief auction officer at Coveted Collections, which means I manage all aspects of the auctions we host for our valued clients, from organizing the invitation list, preparing the items and lots for sale, and overseeing the auction process from start to payment and delivery. There is no auction house like ours. And we're proud of it.

I first learned of the Wine Imports and Distribution Partnership when Payton Alvarez contacted me by email on November 20, YR-1, asking for a proposal to sell a small collection of rare wine. That email is Exhibit 7. I promptly called to say that we would be delighted to assist with a private auction and to obtain the list of wines. That telephone call was on either November 20 or 21. I attended the inspection myself on November 27 to check, appraise, and then estimate the winning bid price for each wine to include in our proposal. I have been organizing auctions and estimating wine values for more than a decade, so I was the only one who needed to attend. I created inspection notes as I prepared the proposal, but I threw those away once I had finalized the proposal for the partnership. We sent a proposal back to Payton quite quickly after that on December 1, YR-1, with all our standard terms, which you can see in Exhibits 7 and 8.

Payton returned the signed proposal a few days later, as you see in Exhibit 7, and we quickly got to work sending invitations to build our bidder list. Two of our favorite bidders, both very interested in wine, were set for a long trip—but they could attend if the auction was held before

December 10, YR-1. We've never organized and executed a private auction in that short of time, but once again Coveted Collections came through and delivered brilliantly for our client.

The auction was held on December 7 at our facility and was a great success. The winning bidders took possession of their wine immediately after the auction, and the net proceeds were deposited in the partnership's bank account the next morning, December 8. Until this lawsuit and being asked to give this deposition under oath, I wasn't aware that anyone was displeased with the auction in any way. You can see the details from the auction in Exhibit 9. To me, it was truly a great success for everyone involved. You can see the amounts of escrow for each bidder who attended the auction, and I can confirm those amounts were pre-paid and deposited before the auction. Any money not spent by the bidders is returned to them within twenty-four hours, as is our policy.

Yes, I am aware that we did not reach all the estimates we provided Payton in Exhibit 8, but I will emphasize exactly what it says in that proposal—those figures are just estimates. Bids can be influenced by so many factors they would fill a book, so you never can tell exactly how a particular item will go until bidding goes live. Some of our estimates were higher than the winning bids, and a few are lower—so that just shows you how foolish it is to try and guess or speculate what the auction price would be for an item, whether public or private auction. Even Parker Roberts wouldn't guarantee estimates, and those estimates are the most accurate on the planet.

Payton never negotiated the fee schedule with us. Candidly, if Payton had, we probably would have given a little bit since I have discretion to reduce the fees to some extent. But Payton never asked. And I certainly wasn't going to offer.

Sure, there were some unforeseen issues that occurred before and during the auction. One high-wealth bidder got into a minor car accident on her way to the auction. She is fine, and I have checked in on her almost daily, but she is in her sixties and was transported to the hospital as a precaution—she was paddle number 5. There was also a typo in the bid catalogue that showed the 1984 red Burgundy as a 1994, but we corrected that several times during the auction. I can assure you no one was confused about the vintage. Yes, I admit a 1994 is significantly less valuable than a 1984, both in terms of age and the growing conditions—there was spectacular weather in 1984 compared to the drought in 1994. But I have no reason to believe that typo had any effect on the bids.

As I mentioned above, we did have to accelerate the timing of the auction since two of our biggest bidders were leaving the country. We have to protect the confidentiality of their names, but you can see them in the bid log as paddle numbers 2 and 6.

We have routinely held wine auctions with fifteen people or less, so I take offense at any suggestion that the number of people in the room had any effect on the final bid price. The ten people at the partnership's auction have more money than 95 percent of those who bid on items at the Allen Virtual Auction House. Trust me. While we did have two others drop out at the last minute, paddle numbers 11 and 12, they were relatively small players. And there are always a few no-shows at a fancy auction. Rich people have things to do.

I believe we raised a spectacular amount for the partnership in this auction given the time pressure, unforeseen issues, and the vagaries in the wine auction market. The variances between the final sale prices and our estimate are normal. While I agree our fees are some of the highest in the industry, and much higher than AVAH's, you get what you pay for. AVAH falls well short of our experience offering rare wine to discerning palates, the close contacts we maintain with wealthy clients, and the prompt payment we guarantee and always deliver to our customers.

Even with all the publicity and allegations in this case, we have continued to offer private wine auctions here in Nita. Since the partnership's auction, we have hosted one additional wine auction. Ten bottles that were sold as part of a probate estate. We spent three weeks planning it, and the total gross sales price was $375,000 with our fees totaling $37,500.

Finally, in the interest of transparency, I want to disclose that paddle number 8 is my brother-in-law. He fancies himself as a wine expert. He has his own money, and I have no involvement in his wine purchase strategies or plans. I did not tell Payton in advance about this because I planned to explain when Payton attended the auction, but Payton was unable to join us for the auction.

I declare under penalty of perjury that the foregoing is true and accurate to the best of my knowledge.

Kondo Mineaux

Dated: January 12, YR-0

Signed and sworn before me on January 12, YR-0

Casey Stamos

Notary Public

IN THE SUPERIOR COURT
IN AND FOR THE COUNTY OF DARROW
AND STATE OF NITA

JORDAN JACOBS Plaintiff,	§ § §	
v.	§	Civil Action No. 95-1984
PAYTON ALVAREZ Defendant.	§ § § §	

DEPOSITION OF COURTNEY GARDNER

I, Courtney Gardner, hereby swear the following statements are true and correct to the best of my knowledge:

My name is Corky Gardner, birth name Courtney, but now everyone calls me Corky. I'm thirty-seven years old, and I've been investing in wine since the day I turned twenty-one. I'm single and have houses here in Nita, Napa Valley, Willamette Valley, and the Finger Lakes region in New York. Wine just fascinates me—culture, history, weather, soil, war, and law are woven into the classic examples of wines from around the world.

Sure, they make Pinot Noir in California just like winemakers in France, but they couldn't taste more distinct. They call it "terroir" (*tay-wahr*), and it means sense of place. Wine from certain places in the world just have this taste, this essence, this terroir. I'm telling you, wine is just so groovy.

I had not heard of the Wine Imports and Distribution Partnership until a month ago, but they weren't in the wine investment and auction scene, and that's where I live, basically. I was invited to and attended the auction of the partnership's wine hosted by Coveted Collections on December 7, YR-1. I was paddle number 3.

To me, the auction was as smooth as a ten-year-old merlot from the gravely soils of Graves in Bordeaux. Don't get brainwashed by *Sideways*, folks. That wine he drinks at the end of the movie out of a Styrofoam cup at the fast-food joint . . . it's merlot! Anyways, I was able to get three amazing bottles of old wine, all well under the estimates I had prepared in advance of the auction. In fact, every bottle other than the Alsatian Riesling went under what I expected them to. I have been to many auctions at Coveted Collections and they do a decent job of making you feel like a rockstar when bidding there. But I don't care about flattery. I care about winning great wines for less than their value. And you can get away with close to robbery when the auction house or other bidders don't know exactly what they're doing.

Let me explain. Coveted Collections tries to keep the number of bidders artificially low. I guess it's to give every invited bidder "a fighting chance," and that's great for the bidders—but not so great for the person who's selling their stuff by auction. Nor is it all that great for Coveted Collections, since I understand their commission is a straight percentage of the winning bid price. Doesn't make a lot of sense to me, like oak on Sauvignon Blanc, but that's another story.

I will agree that the bidders there at the auction, and generally at other Coveted Collection auctions, are very wealthy individuals with cash to spend. More than one or two with far more than me. There are also a few stragglers from time to time, including at the auction on December 7, YR-1. My least favorite bidder who frequents those auctions is the guy with paddle number 8, Kondo's brother-in-law. He is always trying to make a first big bid even though he has little money to actually spend. I've thought in the past about raising a concern to Kondo, since it could appear as if the brother-in-law was trying to juice up the bids, but the final prices ended up so much higher than those early bids that I never did anything about it. But someone might want to look into that.

I can confirm that I listed the 1955 Champagne with AVAH after purchasing it from Coveted Collections. It went far too cheap—most likely because it was foolishly listed as the last item up for bid, after a bunch of cash had already been spent—and I value a good profit over a good bottle of wine any day. I sold the wine with AVAH a few weeks later for $27,600 and took home just over $25,000 in proceeds—what a steal! Kondo's sale left $7,000 just sitting there to be snatched up. I'm telling you, AVAH has some spectacular rates for sellers. I'm not sure if it's always this way, but AVAH offered me $1,000 per bottle plus 5 percent of the final sale price—and that was such a good deal I didn't even attempt to negotiate. That's a first for Corky!

I also recall Kondo and some of the other employees at Coveted Collections telling us there was a minor typo in the catalogue showing the wrong vintage for the red Burgundy. I wouldn't call that a minor typo given the vintage variation between '94 and '84, but no one was confused what they were bidding on. At least I wasn't.

As an experienced expert in wine auctions, I would like to provide my opinion on the general damage the partnership suffered by selling its wine with Coveted Collections instead of AVAH. First, if we assume the final bid prices would've been the same at AVAH, the fees charged by AVAH would've been about half of what Coveted Collections charged. And that amounts to $16,000. But I don't believe that the final bid prices would've been the same. Over the aggregate, I believe the total sale price would have been higher if sold by AVAH. While AVAH had not hosted a rare wine auction at the time, they did so three times shortly after that. I've attended all of them—virtually—and they were excellent. I won some amazing wines and had to battle a bunch of other bidders in the process. I'm sure the returns to the sellers were equally amazing.

I understand trial is set soon in this case. I may be unavailable to testify at the trial because I am departing for an extended trip through Europe.

I declare under penalty of perjury that the foregoing is true and accurate to the best of my knowledge.

Corky Gardner

Dated: January 28, YR-0

Signed and sworn before me on January 28, YR-0

Casey Stamos

Notary Public

Discovery Responses

**IN THE SUPERIOR COURT
IN AND FOR THE COUNTY OF DARROW
AND STATE OF NITA**

JORDAN JACOBS Plaintiff,	§ § §	
v.	§	Civil Action No. 95-1984
PAYTON ALVAREZ Defendant.	§ § § §	

PLAINTIFF'S RESPONSES TO DEFENDANT'S DISCOVERY REQUESTS

Plaintiff Jordan Jacobs responds to Defendant Payton Alvarez's discovery requests as follows:

Request for Admission No. 1: Admit the cost of your flight to France in December YR-1 was higher than any flight you took to any international destination on behalf of the partnership since the partnership's inception.

Response: Admitted.

Request for Admission No. 2: Admit you agreed that the partnership should send a request for proposal to sell the wine collection only to Allen Virtual Auction House and Coveted Collections.

Response: Admitted.

Request for Admission No. 3: Admit you never responded by email to Payton Alvarez's email at the top of Exhibit 11.

Response: Admitted.

Dated: Day of Trial

Respectfully submitted,

WALTON & ASSOCIATES

By: *Olivia W. Walton*

Olivia W. Walton
Attorney for Plaintiff
Nita Bar No. 24144
444 Main Street, Suite 202
Nita City, Nita 99991
(819) 555-3030

IN THE SUPERIOR COURT
IN AND FOR THE COUNTY OF DARROW
AND STATE OF NITA

JORDAN JACOBS Plaintiff,	§ § §	
v.	§	Civil Action No. 95-1984
PAYTON ALVAREZ Defendant.	§ § § §	

DEFENDANT'S RESPONSES TO PLAINTIFF'S DISCOVERY REQUESTS

Defendant Payton Alvarez responds to Plaintiff Jordan Jacobs' discovery requests as follows:

Request for Admission No. 1: Admit selling the partnership's wine collection with Allen Virtual Auction House would have been in the best interest of an orderly dissolution.

Response: Alvarez objects to this request to the extent it suggests only one auction house would have been in the best interest of an orderly dissolution. Subject to and without waiving the foregoing objection—admitted.

Request for Admission No. 2: Admit you did not negotiate the fees with Coveted Collections before signing the proposal in Exhibit 8.

Response: Admitted.

Dated: Day of Trial

Respectfully submitted,
BRUDER LAW

By: *Andrew P. Bruder*

Andrew P. Bruder
Attorney for Defendant
Nita Bar No. 18455
2323 Central Avenue, 12th Floor
Nita City, Nita 99991
(819) 555-8855

EXHIBITS

Exhibit 1

Partnership Agreement of the Wine Imports and Distribution Partnership

This partnership agreement of WINE IMPORTS AND DISTRIBUTION PARTNERSHIP (the "agreement"), a Nita general partnership (the "partnership"), is entered into and shall be effective as of January 1, YR-10, by and among JORDAN JACOBS and PAYTON ALVAREZ (collectively, the "partners") pursuant to the applicable provisions of the Nita Uniform Partnership Code (the "Nita UPC") on the following terms and conditions.

ARTICLE 1
THE PARTNERSHIP

SECTION 1.1. Formation; General Partnership. The partnership was formed as a Nita general partnership under the Nita UPC and the terms and conditions in this agreement.

SECTION 1.2. Name. The name of the partnership shall be Wine Imports and Distribution Partnership (or WIND, pronounced like "wine-d" or what you do to a clock or old watch), and all business of the partnership shall be conducted in such name.

SECTION 1.3. Purpose. The object and purpose of the partnership is to engage in the business of purchasing and importing finished (*i.e.*, bottled) wine and selling the same to retail and hospitality businesses located in the State of Nita. The partnership shall be a partnership only for the purpose specified in the preceding sentence and, except as otherwise provided in this agreement, the partnership shall not engage in any other activity or business and no partner shall have any authority to hold themself out as a general agent of another partner in any other business or activity.

SECTION 1.4. Place of Business. The principal place of business of the partnership shall be located at 2471 Rutherford Road, Nita City, Nita 99990 or at such other place in the State of Nita as may be approved by the partners from time to time.

SECTION 1.5. Term. The term of the partnership commenced on January 1, YR-10, upon the filing of the registration for partnership with the Nita Secretary of State and shall continue until the winding up and liquidation of the partnership as provided herein.

SECTION 1.6. Title to Property. Title to partnership assets, whether real, personal, or mixed and whether tangible or intangible (collectively, "partnership property"), shall be deemed to be owned by the partnership as an entity. No partner, individually or collectively, shall have any ownership interest in partnership property or any portion thereof. Each partner's interest in the partnership shall be personal property for all purposes. The partnership shall hold all partnership property in the name of the partnership and not in the name of any partner.

SECTION 1.7. Payments of Individual Obligations. The partners shall use partnership property and the partnership's credit or lines of credit solely for the benefit of the partnership, and no asset of the partnership shall be transferred or encumbered or in payment of any individual obligation of a partner.

ARTICLE II
PARTNERS; MANAGEMENT; DUTIES

SECTION 2.1. Partners. The names of the partners and the ownership interests allocated to each of the partners are as follows: Jordan Jacobs (50 percent) and Payton Alvarez (50 percent).

SECTION 2.2. Management. Except as otherwise expressly provided in this agreement, the day-to-day business, operations, and affairs of this partnership may be managed by any partner.

SECTION 2.3. Certain Actions. Other than the matters reserved to partners as provided in Sections 2.2 and 2.4, the following decisions or actions shall not be made or taken without the approval of both partners:

(a) The incurrence by the partnership of any indebtedness or the incurrence of any other contractual obligation other than anticipated obligations to pay for routine services and supplies or other obligations incurred in the ordinary course of business;

(b) The sale of a business division of the partnership or a material part of the partnership property or business, the sale of all or substantially all the partnership property or business, or the dissolution of the partnership; or,

(c) The relocation of the partnership's principal place of business.

SECTION 2.4. Partners Authorized to Take Certain Actions on Behalf of the Partnership. Notwithstanding any other requirement in this agreement for unanimous consent of both partners, each partner is authorized to take the following actions and make the following decisions to the extent that such actions and decisions are necessary to permit such partner to carry on the activities of their routine business:

(a) Authorize the partnership to incur incidental expenses and make routine advances that are directly related to the partnership's business;

(b) Cause all filings required to be made pursuant to the Nita UPC to establish and maintain the partnership's status as a general partnership under the Nita UPC to be timely filed; and,

(c) Take any other action and make any other decision that is clearly routine and incidental to the day-to-day conduct of the partnership's business, including reasonable expenses and in-kind donations.

For purposes of illustration only, the partners anticipate the following expenses would be reasonable: (i) offering free tastings of wine; (ii) offering incentives to customers to encourage higher sales; (iii) airfare, hotel costs, and other travel costs to visit international winemakers and vineyards; and (iv) entertainment and hosting expenses, whether for direct or indirect customers—so long as reasonably related to company sales, brand, or reputation.

SECTION 2.5. Consequences of Taking Unauthorized Actions. Notwithstanding anything to the contrary in the Nita UPC, if a partner takes any action or makes any decision for which unanimous consent was required but failed to obtain unanimous consent, that partner shall be personally liable for any damage, costs, or liabilities resulting from the action or decision. A partner's personal liability for any unapproved action or decision shall continue after dissolution of the partnership. If a partner takes any action or makes any decision for which unanimous consent was required but failed to obtain unanimous consent, and such action or decision results in a profit, gain, or other liquidated value to the partnership, that value shall be considered partnership property.

SECTION 2.6. Duties of Partners.

(a) Each partner shall devote their best efforts to serving the partnership and its suppliers and customers in a professional manner;

(b) Each partner shall devote substantially all their normal business time to such services; and,

(c) Each partner shall diligently maintain their fiduciary duties to the partnership, including but not limited to the duties of good faith, fair dealing, loyalty, care, and disclosure.

SECTION 2.7. Approvals. Actions and decisions requiring the unanimous consent of all partners pursuant to any provision of this agreement may be authorized or made either by written consent or a formal vote by both partners. A partner's written consent may be evidenced by their signature on a counterpart of the proposal or by a separate writing (including email communication) that identifies the proposal with reasonable specificity and states that the partner consents to the action or decision.

ARTICLE III
BOOKS AND RECORDS

SECTION 3.1. Books and Records. The partnership shall maintain at its principal place of business separate books and records of the partnership that show a true and accurate record of all costs and expenses incurred, all charges made, all credits made and received, and all income derived in connection with the conduct of the partnership and the operation of the partnership business in accordance with this agreement.

ARTICLE IV
DISSOLUTION AND WINDING UP

SECTION 4.1. Liquidating Events. The partnership shall dissolve and commence winding up and liquidating upon the first to occur of any of the following ("liquidating events"):

(a) The decision of both partners to dissolve, wind up, and liquidate the partnership;

(b) The sale of all or substantially all the partnership property or business or the happening of any other event that makes it unlawful or impossible to carry on the business of the partnership; or,

(c) Any event which causes there to be only one partner.

The partners hereby agree that, notwithstanding any provision of the Nita UPC, the partnership shall not dissolve prior to the occurrence of a liquidating event. If it is determined, by a court of competent jurisdiction, that the partnership has dissolved prior to the occurrence of a liquidating event, the partners hereby agree to continue the business of the partnership without winding up or liquidation.

SECTION 4.2. Winding Up. Upon the occurrence of a liquidating event, the partnership shall continue solely for the purpose of winding up its affairs in an orderly manner, liquidating its assets, and satisfying the claims of its creditors and partners. No partner shall take any action that is inconsistent with, or not necessary to or appropriate for, winding up the partnership's business and affairs. To the extent not inconsistent with the foregoing, all covenants contained in this agreement and obligations provided for in this agreement shall continue to be fully binding on the partners until such time as the partnership property has been distributed pursuant to this Article IV and the partnership has terminated. All partners shall be responsible for overseeing the winding up and liquidation of the partnership, shall take full account of the partnership's liabilities and partnership property, shall cause the partnership property to be liquidated promptly and consistent with Section 806 of the Nita UPC, and shall cause the proceeds therefrom, to the extent sufficient therefore, to be applied and distributed in the following order:

(a) First, to creditors other than partners in satisfaction of all the partnership's debts and liabilities to such creditors;

(b) Second, to the partners in satisfaction of all the partnership's debts and liabilities to partners; and,

(c) Finally, the balance (if any) to the partners in equal payments.

SECTION 4.3. Liquidation. In liquidating the partnership property for purposes of winding up the partnership's business upon the occurrence of a liquidating event, the assets of the partnership may be disposed of by public or private sale. Liquidation or distribution of the partnership's assets may be deferred for a reasonable time if an immediate sale or distribution of all or some of the partnership's assets would be impractical or would cause an undue delay or unreasonable loss to the partners. The decision as to the liquidation or distribution method/vendor of the partnership's assets must always be in the best interest of an orderly dissolution consistent with Section 806 of the Nita UPC.

ARTICLE V
MISCELLANEOUS

SECTION 5.1. Notice. All notices and other communications under this agreement shall be in writing and shall be deemed given (a) when delivered personally by hand, (b) when sent by email, or (c) one business day following the day sent by overnight courier, if to the partnership, to the partnership at the address set forth in Section 1.4, or to such other address as the partnership may from time to time specify by notice to the partners; if to a partner, to such partner at their partnership email address.

SECTION 5.2. Binding Effect. Except as otherwise provided in this agreement, every covenant, term, and provision of this agreement shall be binding upon and inure to the benefit of the partners and their respective heirs, legatees, legal representatives, successors, transferees, and assigns.

SECTION 5.3. Construction. Every covenant, term, and provision of this agreement shall be construed simply according to its fair meaning and not strictly for or against any partner.

SECTION 5.4. Headings. Sections and other headings contained in this agreement are for reference purposes only and are not intended to describe, interpret, define, or limit the scope, extent, or intention of this agreement or any provision hereof.

SECTION 5.5. Severability. Except as otherwise provided in the succeeding sentence, every provision of this agreement is intended to be severable, and if any term or provision is illegal or invalid for any reason whatsoever, such illegality or invalidity shall not affect the validity or legality of the remainder of this agreement. The preceding sentence of this Section 5.5 shall be of no force or effect if the consequence of enforcing the remainder of this agreement without such illegal or invalid term or provision would be to cause any partner to lose the benefit of their economic bargain.

SECTION 5.6. Further Action. Each partner agrees to perform all further acts and execute, acknowledge, and deliver any documents that may be reasonably necessary, appropriate, or desirable to carry out the provisions of this agreement.

SECTION 5.7. Governing Law. The laws of the State of Nita shall govern the validity of this agreement, the construction of its terms, and the interpretation of the rights and duties of the partners.

Jordan Jacobs

Dated: December 30, YR-11

Payton Alvarez

Dated: December 30, YR-11

Exhibit 2

Settlement Agreement

This settlement agreement (the "agreement") by and between JORDAN JACOBS and PAYTON ALVAREZ, the partners of the soon-to-be dissolved WINE IMPORTS AND DISTRIBUTION PARTNERSHIP (the "partnership"), is entered into and shall be effective as of November 1, YR-1, on the following terms and conditions:

WHEREAS, Jacobs and Alvarez wish to expedite the voluntary dissolution of the partnership;

WHEREAS, the dissolution process is complete except for two outstanding items, and the current cash balance of the partnership is $505,800.00; and,

WHEREAS, there are two outstanding items to be resolved before the cash balance of the partnership can be equally divided and the partnership is formally terminated.

NOW THEREFORE, the partners agree as follows:

SECTION 1.1. Wine Collection. Alvarez shall be responsible for preparing a request for proposal to be sent to potential auction houses with the capability of selling the partnership's wine collection. Alvarez shall also be responsible for vetting and selecting the auction house to sell the wine collection; provided, however, that Alvarez expressly agrees that any final decision on the auction house must be in the best interest of an orderly dissolution as provided by the relevant Nita UPC and the partnership agreement.

SECTION 1.2. French Purchase Contracts. Jacobs shall be responsible for traveling to France and resolving the two purchase contracts that must be terminated as part of the voluntary dissolution process. Jacobs shall also be responsible for negotiating and executing any agreement to terminate those contracts; provided, however, that Jacobs must obtain Alvarez's express written consent if the total of those agreements (including compensation to be paid and expenses incurred in the process) is more than $75,000. Jacobs is still obligated to ensure that the amounts incurred are reasonable and necessary.

SECTION 1.3. All Other Dissolution Matters. Other than the items referenced in Sections 1.1 and 1.2, the partners hereby agree that all other assets and liabilities (as used in the broadest sense) related to liquidation and dissolution have been resolved and accounted for in the current cash balance. The partners expressly release any complaint, objection, cause of action, or the like related to any aspect of the partnership or the dissolution process other than the issues referenced in Sections 1.1 and 1.2.

SECTION 1.4. Right to Sue for Breach of This Agreement. Notwithstanding anything herein to the contrary, the partners expressly agree that each partner retains the right to sue or seek redress for any breach of this agreement, whether by direct cause of action, counterclaim, or offset/setoff, for two years from the effective date of this settlement agreement.

SECTION 1.5 Limitations of this Settlement Agreement. Unless expressly addressed in this settlement agreement, the rights and obligations set forth in the partnership agreement shall be unaffected by this settlement agreement.

Jordan Jacobs	*Payton Alvarez*
Dated: November 1, YR-1	Dated: November 1, YR-1

Exhibit 3

Notice of Termination of Partnership

NITA SECRETARY OF STATE

DIVISION OF ENTITY REGISTRATION (CORPORATIONS, PARTNERSHIPS)

Filing Date:	December 11, YR-1
Filer:	Payton Alvarez, Partner
Document No.:	NOT-725441
Entity:	Wine Imports and Distribution Partnership (Entity No.: W6LM)

NOTICE OF TERMINATION

NOTICE IS HEREBY GIVEN

The Wine Imports and Distribution Partnership, a Nita partnership, has ceased operations and terminated its existence as of the date of this filing.

The partnership has no further business, assets, or liabilities. Any persons claiming otherwise are not authorized and do not represent the partnership.

Signed,

Payton Alvarez

Payton Alvarez—on behalf of the now-terminated and previously existing Wine Imports and Distribution Partnership

Exhibit 4

Notice of Registration

NITA SECRETARY OF STATE

DIVISION OF ENTITY REGISTRATION (CORPORATIONS, PARTNERSHIPS)

Filing Date:	December 31, YR-11
Filer:	Jordan Jacobs & Payton Alvarez, Partners
Document No.:	NOR-0245117
Entity:	Wine Imports and Distribution Partnership

NOTICE OF REGISTRATION

NOTICE IS HEREBY GIVEN

The Wine Imports and Distribution Partnership has registered with the Nita Secretary of State to conduct business in the State of Nita. Jordan Jacobs and Payton Alvarez are the only partners of the partnership, and they each own 50 percent interest in the partnership. A copy of the partnership agreement governing the partnership is available upon legitimate request.

The purpose of the partnership is to import finished/bottled wine from European countries (namely France, Italy, and Spain) and distribute the same to retailers (restaurants, bars, package stores) in the State of Nita. The partnership has obtained all necessary permits, authorizations, and approvals to conduct its business.

The partnership's business address is: 2471 Rutherford Road, Nita City, Nita 99990.

Electronically signed: /s/ Jordan Jacobs; /s/ Payton Alvarez

Do not type or mark below this line—for Nita Secretary of State use ONLY

Entity No. Assigned:	W6LM
Effective Date of Partnership:	January 1, YR-10
Secretary of State Approval:	Zain Bahar Secretary of State, Nita

Exhibit 5

Email Exchange Between Alvarez and AVAH (November YR-1)

Payton Alvarez

From:	riley@avah.nita
To:	Alvarez, Payton <payton.alvarez@wind.nita>; Jacobs, Jordan <jordan.jacobs@wind.nita>
Subject:	RE: Request for Proposal—8 bottle rare wine collection
Date:	November 30, YR-1 8:22 AM
Attachment:	AVAH RFP Response to WIND Partnership.pdf

Dear Payton & Jordan:

The Allen Virtual Auction House is pleased to respond to your request for proposal with the attached proposal. Please contact me once you have reviewed so we can discuss how we can best serve you.

All the best—Cheers!
Riley Allen
CEO—Allen Virtual Auction House (AVAH)

From:	Alvarez, Payton <payton.alvarez@wind.nita>
To:	Alvarez, Payton <payton.alvarez@wind.nita>; Jacobs, Jordan <jordan.jacobs@wind.nita>
Subject:	Request for Proposal—8 bottle rare wine collection
Date:	November 20, YR-1 4:42 PM

Dear recipients:

The Wine Imports and Distribution Partnership is going through a voluntary dissolution to cease all operations. The partnership owns eight bottles of rare and highly valuable wine that we would like to sell by auction as soon as practicable.

We have set aside November 27 from 10am to 4pm for you, your appraiser, and any other consultants to come by and inspect the physical bottles. Please let us know if you require a different day or time, and please contact me by phone if you would like to know more about the wines before that visit. My direct line is (819) 555-2839.

In your proposal, please specially provide us with an estimated sale price (or range) for each bottle of wine, a detailed explanation of your fees and other expenses, the time we can expect to receive the funds at the conclusion of the auction, and any other details about your auction house or approach to selling this collection that would be useful for our consideration.

If you have any questions, please feel free to contact me.
Thank you.

Payton Alvarez
Chief Distribution Officer
Wine Imports and Distribution Partnership

Exhibit 6

RFP Response from Allen Virtual Auction House (November 30, YR-1)

ALLEN VIRTUAL
Auction House

November 30, YR-1

Payton Alvarez
Wine Imports and Distribution Partnership
2471 Rutherford Road
Nita City, Nita 99990
payton.alvarez@wind.nita
Sent via email

Re: Request for Proposal sent via email on November 20, YR-1

Dear Payton:

We are humbled and excited that you contacted us requesting a proposal to sell your incredibly impressive, rare wine collection at our public auction house. As you may not be aware, we have recently invested substantial time and money to enhance our capabilities to auction different types of assets that our customers are looking for. Wine, especially rare wine, is precisely one of the markets we've been eager to get into. We would be proud to partner with you on that maiden voyage!

Thank you again for setting aside time for me, our appraiser, and our wine fraud expert to come by and physically inspect the wine on November 27, YR-1. That was extremely helpful in allowing us to not only evaluate and appraise your wine but also get a great sense of you and your partnership.

We are delighted to respond to your proposal as follows:

- Items/Lots—Eight bottles of rare wine to be listed as separate items during a special online auction dedicated exclusively to your wine collection. The "bid clock" will reset to ten seconds after each new bid.
- Order of Auction—we will analyze your wines against recent auction and wine exchange data to determine the most profitable order your wines should appear during the auction.
- Advertising—we commit to spending $7,500 in advertising, marketing, and promotions in the one to two weeks prior to the online auction, an amount that will not be passed on to you.
- Appraisals/Fraud Check—our fraud consultant has concluded there is no evidence that any of your bottles are fraudulent, which was bolstered by the diligent provenance documentation you provided. This consultant and our appraiser (who assisted with the estimates below) are also free of charge.

- Fees—we have proposed a reduced fee rate for this auction of $1,000 per bottle plus 5 percent of the winning bid price. This is reduced from our standard rates of $2,500 per item or 15 percent of winning bid price, whichever is higher.
- Non-Payment—if a winning bidder fails to pay for any item won, we will attempt to sell the item to the next-highest bidder at their last bid price. If that is unsuccessful, we will return the item to you without any charge.
- Bidders/Users—we cannot guarantee the number of users who will log into your auction, but you reserve the right to postpone the auction if there are less than 100 users logged into the auction platform at the start time. We have performed no vetting of the users who register and attend the auction.

Estimated Range for Winning Bids & Mandatory Minimum Floor

**Please note these are only estimated ranges and do not indicate a promise or guarantee of the actual winning bids for any item in any respect

**Mandatory Minimum Floor pricing means bids must surpass this amount before you are obligated to sell the wine to the highest bidder.

Vintage	Wine	Estimated Range of Winning Bid	Minimum Floor
1943	Alsace Riesling	$37,000 to $40,000	$25,000
1885	Y'Quem	$35,000 to $38,000	$17,500
1919	Rioja	$31,000 to $34,000	$17,500
1984	Red Burgundy	$25,000 to $28,000	$15,000
1919	German Riesling	$25,000 to $28,000	$15,000
1955	Champagne	$20,000 to $23,000	$10,000
1977	Bordeaux	$9,000 to $12,000	$4,000
1990	Napa Cabernet	$6,000 to $9,000	$2,500

Thank you again for the opportunity to partner with you in selling your rare wine collection as part of your dissolution process. If you agree, please sign below.

We cannot wait to get started!

Riley Allen

CEO—Allen Virtual Auction House (AVAH)

Accepted and Agreed by: ____________________________ on Date: _____________

Exhibit 7

Email Exchange Between Alvarez and Kondo (November/December YR-1)

Payton Alvarez

From:	Alvarez, Payton <payton.alvarez@wind.nita>
To:	Kondo@CovetedCollections.nita
Subject:	RE: Request for Proposal—8 bottle rare wine collection
Date:	December 3, YR-1 6:35 PM
Attachment:	Coveted Collection RFP Response (SIGNED).pdf

See attached.

Payton Alvarez
Chief Distribution Officer
Wine Imports and Distribution Partnership

From:	Kondo@CovetedCollections.nita
To:	Alvarez, Payton <payton.alvarez@wind.nita>; Jacobs, Jordan <jordan.jacobs@wind.nita>
Subject:	RE: Request for Proposal—8 bottle rare wine collection
Date:	December 1, YR-1 1:15 PM
Attachment:	Coveted Collection RFP Response.pdf

Dear Payton Alvarez:

Please find our response to your request for proposal attached to this email. Please let us know if you have any questions, and we truly hope to serve you in an auction of your priceless wine collection.

Truly Yours,

Kondo Mineaux
Owner and Chief Auction Officer

From:	Alvarez, Payton <payton.alvarez@wind.nita>
To:	Alvarez, Payton <payton.alvarez@wind.nita>; Jacobs, Jordan <jordan.jacobs@wind.nita>
Subject:	Request for Proposal—8 bottle rare wine collection
Date:	November 20, YR-1 4:42 PM

Dear recipients:

The Wine Imports and Distribution Partnership is going through a voluntary dissolution to cease all operations. The partnership owns eight bottles of rare and highly valuable wine that we would like to sell by auction as soon as practicable.

We have set aside November 27 from 10am to 4pm for you, your appraiser, and any other consultants to come by and inspect the physical bottles. Please let us know if you require a different day or time, and please contact me by phone if you would like to know more about the wines before that visit. My direct line is (819) 555-2839.

In your proposal, please specially provide us with an estimated sale price (or range) for each bottle of wine, a detailed explanation of your fees and other expenses, the time we can expect to receive the funds at the conclusion of the auction, and any other details about your auction house or approach to selling this collection that would be useful for our consideration.

If you have any questions, please feel free to contact me.

Thank you.

Payton Alvarez
Chief Distribution Officer
Wine Imports and Distribution Partnership

RFP Response from Coveted Collections (December 1, YR-1)

Coveted Collections
Nita's premier auction house
858 Elm Drive
Nita City, Nita 99992

December 1, YR-1

Dear Payton Alvarez:

Thank you again for giving us the opportunity to sell your impressive wine collection at Coveted Collections. This letter will serve as our formal response to your request for proposal sent via email on November 20, YR-1.

Enclosed please find an estimated price range for each bottle that has been prepared based on our physical inspection of the wine, consultation with our appraisers and other experts, and industry knowledge of the rare wine market and potential buyers. Please note that the estimates below are only estimates—they in no way guarantee or promise a sale price within that price range.

Should you agree to our proposal, please sign below to confirm your acceptance. We anticipate that we can host a private auction with at least a dozen high-net-worth individuals within one week (subject to any availability concerns from those potential buyers).

Sincerely,

Kondo Mineaux

Kondo Mineaux
Owner and Chief Auction Officer

****I have read the proposal and all of its attachments, and I agree to the terms contained herein on behalf of the Wine Imports and Distribution Partnership:

Payton Alvarez Dec. 3, YR-1

Payton Alvarez

Estimated Sale Range (Wine Imports and Distribution Partnership)

1977 Bordeaux	$ 12,500 – $ 15,000
1919 German Riesling	$22,500 – $ 25,000
1990 Napa Cab	$ 8,000 – $ 12,000
1984 Red Burgundy	$22,500 – $ 25,000
1943 Alsace Riesling	$30,000 – $ 35,000
1919 Rioja	$30,000 – $ 35,000
1885 Y'Quem	$35,000 – $ 40,000
1955 Champagne	$25,000 – $ 30,000

Fees & Expenses

You are responsible for paying all fees and expenses associated with the auction as described herein, all of which will be debited against the gross proceeds raised from the auction before payment to you.

Fees—we charge a flat 18 percent of the final sale price for each bottle of wine.

Taxes—we will deduct the local 8 percent tax rate from the net proceeds (gross sales price less our fees).

Expenses—you will not be charged for the costs of our appraiser and other expert consultants, nor will you bear the cost of the auction itself. You shall be responsible for all other expenses.

The Auction

We are Nita's premier private auction house with more than 1,500 auctions hosted by Coveted Collections in the last ten years. We strive to provide the most upscale auction experience possible with curated bidders specifically chosen for your particular asset.

All the individuals who attend the auction will be required to deposit funds in escrow for use during the auction. This not only ensures that your buyers have sufficient funds but also allows us to collect payment immediately after the auction and send the net proceeds to you shortly thereafter.

We guarantee that you will receive the net proceeds from your auction within seventy-two hours after conclusion of the auction. In the unlikely event we fail to meet this guarantee, we will pay you 2 percent interest on your net proceeds for every day after the seventy-two-hour window until paid to you.

You will also be provided with an automated bid log showing you the bidders (by paddle number) and bids for each asset for confirmation. You are also invited to attend the auction, should you wish.

Exhibit 9

Final Invoice from Coveted Collections (December 8, YR-1)

Coveted Collections
Nita's premier auction house
858 Elm Drive
Nita City, Nita 99992

December 8, YR-1

Payton Alvarez
Wine Imports and Distribution Partnership
2471 Rutherford Road
Nita City, Nita 99990
Sent by email

Dear Payton Alvarez:

Thank you again for choosing to sell your impressive wine collection with us. Below please find a summary of the winning bids for each wine and the details regarding taxes and our fees. The total net amount we will deposit into your bank account is $135,414.80 USD. We expect that to appear in your bank account tomorrow morning.

I have also attached the automated bid tracking log that we used during the auction, should you be curious about the bidding for each item.

Thank you again for choosing Coveted Collections, Nita's premier auction house and grateful host for your completed auction.

Sincerely,

Kondo Mineaux

Kondo Mineaux
Owner and Chief Auction Officer

(Enclosures—Final Auction Invoice & Auto Bid Log)

Final Auction Invoice (Wine Imports and Distribution Partnership)

Auction Item	Sale Price	Fees (18%)
1977 Bordeaux	$ 11,000.00	$ 1,980.00
1919 German Riesling	$ 28,000.00	$ 5,040.00
1990 Napa Cab	$ 6,500.00	$ 1,170.00
1984 Red Burgundy	$ 23,000.00	$ 4,140.00
1943 Alsace Riesling	$ 38,000.00	$ 6,840.00
1919 Rioja	$ 27,000.00	$ 4,860.00
1885 Y'Quem	$ 28,000.00	$ 5,040.00
1955 Champagne	$ 18,000.00	$ 3,240.00
	$ 179,500.00	**$32,310.00**
Subtotal	**$ 147,190.00**	
Taxes (8%)	($ 11,775.20)	
TOTAL PAYMENT	**$ 135,414.80**	

Automated Bid Tracking Log
Auction Date: December 7, YR-1
Seller: Wine Imports and Distribution Partnership, Wine (9btl) #W5771
Location: Coveted Collections
Last Software Update: January 1, YR-3

[Items/Lots]

No.	Item Description
1	1977 Bordeaux
2	1919 German Riesling
3	1990 Napa Cab
4	1984 Red Burgundy
5	1943 Alsace Riesling
6	1919 Rioja
7	1885 Y'Quem
8	1955 Champagne

[Bidders]

Paddle	Escrow	
#1	$ 100,000	
#2	$ 250,000	
#3	$ 150,000	
#4	$ 75,000	
#5	$ 450,000	
#6	$ 150,000	
#7	$ 150,000	
#8	$ 15,000	
#9	$ 30,000	
#10	$ 10,000	
#11	$ 25,000	
#12	$ 25,000	
#13	$ 45,000	

No. 1—1977 Bordeaux

Open	– $ 2,500
#8	– $ 3,500
#3	– $ 5,000
#7	– $ 6,000
#1	– $ 7,500
#3	– $ 8,500
#7	– $10,000
#1	– $10,500
#7	– $11,000
SOLD	– $11,000 (#7)

No. 2—1919 Riesling

Open	– $ 5,000
#2	– $ 5,000
#3	– $ 7,500
#6	– $10,000
#2	– $12,500
#6	– $15,000
#3	– $17,500
#6	– $18,500
#2	– $20,000
#1	– $22,500
#6	– $25,000
#2	– $26,000
#1	– $27,000
#2	– $27,500
#1	– $28,000
SOLD	– $28,000 (#1)

No. 3—1990 Napa Cab

Open	– $ 1,000
#10	– $ 2,000
#13	– $ 2,500
#3	– $ 4,000
#10	– $ 5,000
#8	– $ 6,000
#10	– $ 6,500
SOLD	– $ 6,500 (#10)

No. 4—1984 Red Burgundy

Open	– $ 5,000
#8	– $ 7,500
#4	– $ 9,000
#8	– $10,000
#4	– $11,000
#3	– $12,500
#4	– $15,000
#3	– $18,000
#4	– $20,000
#3	– $22,000
#4	– $22,500
#3	– $25,000
SOLD	– $25,000 (#3)

No. 5—1943 Alsace Riesling

Open	– $ 5,000
#8	– $10,000
#6	– $12,500
#2	– $15,000
#6	– $17,500
#2	– $18,500
#3	– $20,000
#2	– $25,000
#6	– $30,000
#2	– $35,000
#6	– $37,000
#2	– $38,000
SOLD	– $38,000 (#2)

No. 6—1919 Rioja

Open	– $ 5,000
#8	– $12,500
#1	– $13,500
#3	– $15,000
#1	– $17,500
#3	– $20,000
#1	– $25,000
#3	– $27,000
SOLD	– $27,000 (#3)

No. 7—1885 Y'Quem

Open	– $ 5,000
#8	– $10,000
#3	– $15,000
#7	– $20,000
#3	– $22,500
#9	– $24,000
#3	– $25,000
#9	– $26,000
#3	– $26,500
#9	– $26,750
#7	– $27,000
#9	– $27,500
SOLD	– $28,000 (#9)

No. 8—1955 Champagne

Open	– $ 5,000
#8	– $ 7,500
#3	– $10,000
#8	– $12,500
#3	– $14,500
#6	– $16,000
#4	– $17,000
#3	– $17,500
#6	– $17,750
#3	– $18,000
SOLD	– $18,000 (#3)

Verified and confirmed by:

Kondo Mineaux

Dec. 7, YR-1 (6:30pm)

Kondo Mineaux
Owner and Chief Auction Officer

Exhibit 10

Text from Payton Alvarez's Phone (December 2, YR-1, at 6:02 p.m.)

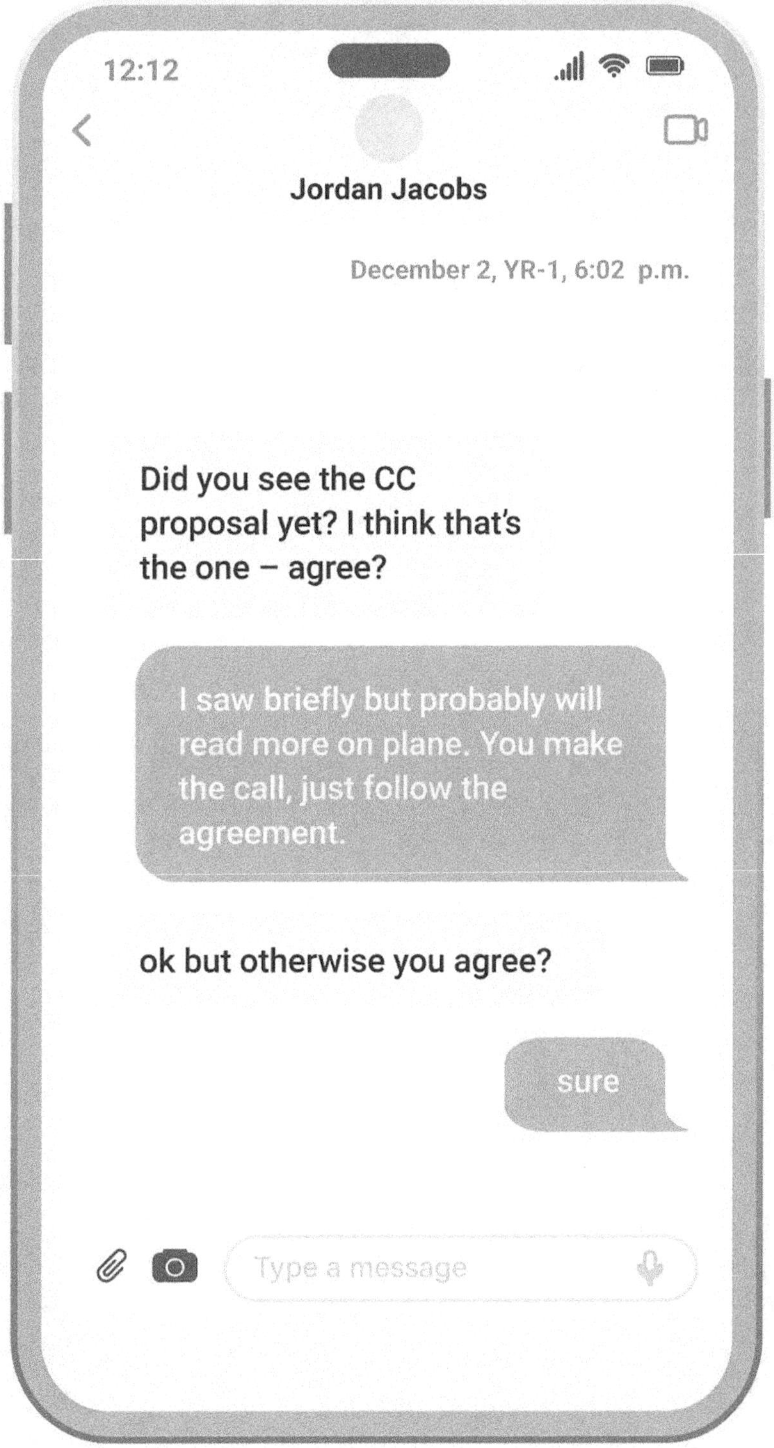

Exhibit 11

Email Exchange Between Jacobs and Alvarez (December YR-1)

Payton Alvarez

From: Alvarez, Payton <payton.alvarez@wind.nita>
To: Jacobs, Jordan <jordan.jacobs@wind.nita>
Subject: RE: Receipts & Auction
Date: December 11, YR-1 6:14:15 AM

Received. I will file the Notice of Termination with the Secretary of State at the end of the day today unless you have any objection or concerns.

~Payton

From: Jacobs, Jordan <jordan.jacobs@wind.nita>
Sent: Thursday, December 11, YR-1 1:13 AM
To: Alvarez, Payton <payton.alvarez@wind.nita>
Subject: RE: Receipts & Auction
Attachments: Burgundy Expense Report (Dec YR-1).pdf; Veronique Check.pdf; Rolande Check.pdf

See attached per your request.
JJ

From: Alvarez, Payton <payton.alvarez@wind.nita>
To: Jacobs, Jordan <jordan.jacobs@wind.nita>
Subject: Receipts & Auction
Date: December 10, YR-1 2:14:15 PM
Attachment: Final Invoice (Wine Imports and Distribution Partnership).pdf

JJ—
Look, I don't know why you're getting all worked up over the auction. We needed it to happen. You resolved the contracts. Now we get to split the cash. Attached is everything about the auction.

I'll make you a deal—just send me the expense report and copies of the checks from the trip. I'll agree to them without question and take no issue with any of your obligations under any of our agreements if you say OK to the Cov Col auction. Ok?

Payton Alvarez
Chief Distribution Officer
Wine Imports and Distribution Partnership

Exhibit 12

Check from Partnership to Domaine Veronique et fils

Wine Imports and Distribution Partnership
Jordan Jacobs, Partner
2471 Rutherford Rd.
Nita City, Nita 99990

COMPANY CHECK

Date Dec. 5, YR-1

Pay to the Order Of Domaine Veronique et fils

USD $19,000.00

Nineteen thousand US dollars and 0/100..

Memo Termination of purchase contract

Jordan Jacobs

222107888 543008282 Check 140

Exhibit 13

Check from Partnership to Chateau Rolande

Wine Imports and Distribution Partnership
Jordan Jacobs, Partner
2471 Rutherford Rd.
Nita City, Nita 99990

COMPANY CHECK **Date** Dec. 8, YR-1

Pay to the Order Of Chateau Rolande USD $22,500.00

Twenty-two thousand five hundred US dollars and 0/100..

Memo Termination of purchase contract

Jordan Jacobs

222107888 543008282 Check 141

Exhibit 14

Expense Report (December YR-1)

EXPENSE REPORT

Destination: Beaune, France	Duration: 9 days
Arrival: December 3, YR-1	Departure: December 10, YR-1

Hotel Address: Relais Beaune, 717 Domaine Ave, Beaune, FR 11111 *Junior Suite, 8 nights ($1259/night); Complimentary Breakfast, Parking, Daily Champagne
Transportation: Rental Car from CDG Paris Airport *Paris Car Rental (Counter G); Req. Mercedes AMG Convertible; 8 Days ($885.95/day); Return by 12pm ($100.00 per hour thereafter)

Date:	Event(s) & Expenses:	$ Amount:
Dec 2	Round trip airfare: FlyFrance #62, Business Class (Seat 3A) Departure 6:40pm local; Arrival 7:55am (Dec 3) local	$11,450.75
Dec 3	Arrival at CDG Paris 7:40am; Retrieve rental car; drive Paris to Beaune	$ 7,087.60
	Check in at Relais Beaune	$10,072.00
	Dinner at Hotel Restaurant	$ 145.00
Dec 4	Drive Beaune to Dijon; Meeting with Frederic	$ 308.50
	**Hotel in Dijon ($220/night) for 1 night;	
	Dinner – $88.50	
Dec 5	**Breakfast with Frederic – $44.00; drive Dijon to Beaune	$ 483.00
	Lunch – $35.00; drive Beaune to Dijon	
	Dinner with Frederick – $404.00; drive Dijon to Beaune	
Dec 6	Drive into Burgundy; Meeting with Jerome **Free day	$ 345.00
	Lunch – $110.00; Winery Tours – $80.00; Dinner – $155.00	
Dec 7	Lunch meeting with Jerome; Lunch – $145.00	
	Dinner – $241.00	$ 386.00
Dec 8	Lunch – $21.00	
	Dinner with Jerome & Camille – $550.00	$ 571.00

Dec 9	Check out; Drive Beaune to Paris; Lunch – \$48.00; Gas – \$125.00 **Check in Paris Airport Hotel (\$110/night); Dinner – \$75.00	\$ 358.00
Dec 10	Departure: 8:05am local; FlyFrance #33, Business Class (Seat 4A) Arrival at Nita Int'l Airport at 10:45am local	\$ NA
	Total Expenses for Reimbursement:	**\$31,206.85**

APPROVED BY: ____________________ *DATED:* ____________________

Exhibit 15

Vine Acuity Blog Page (October 15, YR-1)

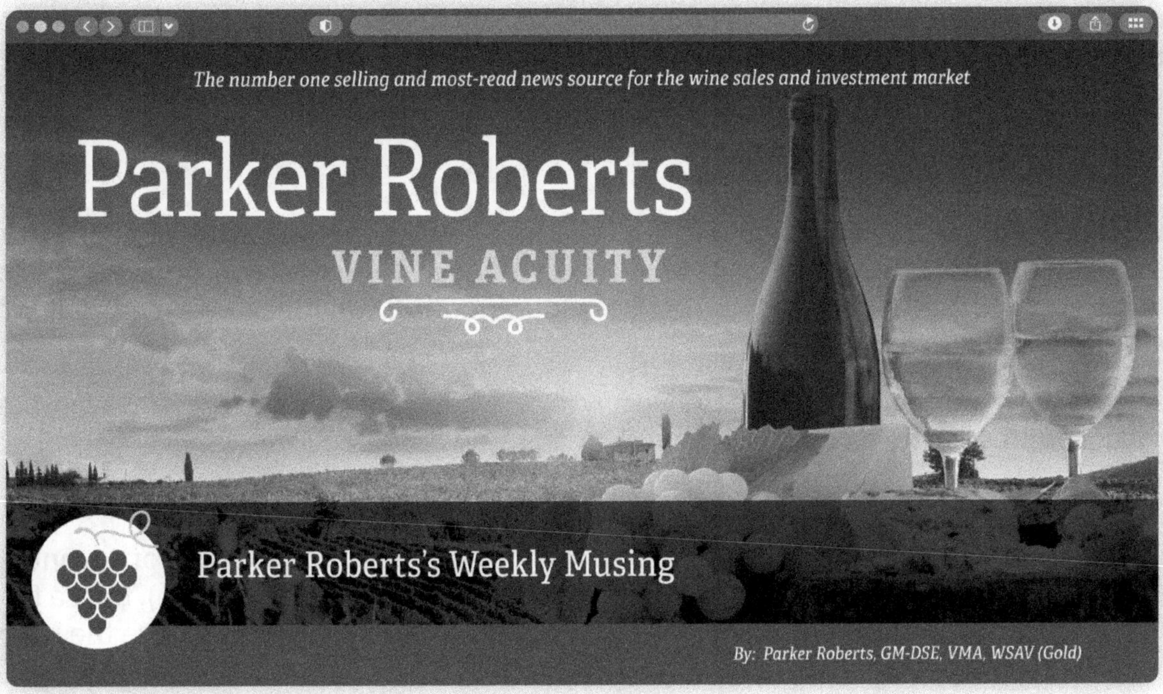

October 15, YR-1

This week, I decided to go into my Q&A inbox to find some inspiration for the column. For those of you who are new here, there's a page on my website where you can submit questions for me to answer, which I occasionally do on social media—but only if they're perplexing or make me laugh. Here's a gem:

From Marc G. in Nita Bay, Nita

> My dad recently passed away. While we were cleaning out his house, I discovered a humidor refrigerator thing in his office with six bottles of old wine inside. I showed photos of the bottles to a local private auction house and was floored at their estimated sale price (and eagerness to sell it). Here is a list of the wines: [REDACTED]. We could really use the money. My wife and I still are carrying quite a bit of debt from law school, and we'd love to pay it all off. Or should we shop around?

First of all, Marc, I'm terribly sorry for your loss.

Getting rid of investment-grade wine that you don't want and are eager to sell presents an interesting situation. (I redacted the wine list to protect Marc's privacy as a few of them were indeed quite magnificent and because I may try to buy a few!). Your reference to law school gave me the idea to phone a friend I ran into many years ago. Nicola is a bankruptcy attorney who's seen her fair share of asset sales, liquidations, auctions, and the like. We chatted just briefly, but she directed me to a statute in the Nita Uniform Partnership Code with this phrase: "the best interest of an orderly dissolution." Nicola explained that comes up when a company has to sell all its assets because it's gone under, and the folks making the decisions on how to sell it or where to sell it have to ensure their decisions are in the best interest of an orderly dissolution.

Um, Parker, I thought this was an article about wine.

It is, I'm almost there.

The rest of the statute has a bunch of legalese that I won't bore you with, but it has three categories of things to consider: (1) how much money you make from the sale; (2) how quickly you get that money in your bank account; and (3) anything unique about what you're selling.

Marc, while I'm certainly not going to give any legal analysis to you, I figured this legal standard could prove to be a useful framework to answer your question.

Money Raised

This appears the most important one to you. Private auctions can have a lot of advantages here because they can have curated lists of bidders (especially for rare wine), host a fancy event to drum up the bidding (at least in theory), and ensure your buyers have the money (such as requiring escrow deposits).

The downside is that you only have a roomful of people bidding on your wine whereas there might be thousands of people online for a high-profile public auction. The question is, how many of those people have the wherewithal to purchase, say, a $20,000 bottle of old Bordeaux?

But don't forget you actually only care about the number that hits your bank account. Private houses charge much higher fees than the public auctions. Sure, you get value in return for those fees, but it's a personal call whether you think it's worth it.

Another point that people often miss is that private auction houses have some risk because there is typically no guaranteed floor price whereas public auctions almost always have a minimum bid before the asset will be sold. So, there's less of a guarantee at private auctions, and it can be rather unnerving to watch a bottle worth an estimated $20k open at something like $5k before the bidding starts.

When It Hits the Bank Account

Private auctions win here, too. Some promise to get you paid within twenty-four hours of the auction, and I've been told on more than one occasion that it is true. Public auctions will get you paid in a week or two, but the biggest risk here is the chance your winning bidder can't pay. Public auctions will still vet the bidders for the most expensive items, rare wine included, but just because they can pay doesn't mean they always do pay. If the buyer ghosts the auction house, they might try to sell it to the next highest bidder, but that is never certain. And if that doesn't work, they'll just hand the wine back to you—not something you want.

Special Stuff

Wine is a tough resale market when you're hoping for five figures per bottle. You need a wealthy, willing bidder who wants that particular type of wine, is willing to take the risk of spoilage (especially if it's decades old), and, frankly, physically shows up to the auction. Tastes are unpredictable, predictions fluctuate, opinions change about the best old vintages. All part of the wine game.

As for you Marc, based on the wine list you gave me and the proposal from the private auction house, I would say shop around and aggressively negotiate on fees and expenses. That doesn't mean a public auction will be in your "best interests," or that a private one won't.

But if there's twenty-five or even fifty thousand dollars more out there at an alternative, I suspect you'd trade a week or two of waiting for that.

Be sure to check out my updated wine valuations available on my website under the tab "Wine Valuations." They are my personal evaluations for the price of almost every valuable wine out there.

Cheers! (and let me know when that auction is!)

Parker

Exhibit 16

Wine Valuations from Vine Acuity Website (October 15, YR-1)

PARKER ROBERTS VINE ACUITY - SELECTED WINE VALUATIONS											
As of Oct. 15 of each year listed below - Last updated Oct. 15, YR-1											
Wine		**Historical Estimated Value** (in thousands - USD) (Good Condition / Pristine Condition)									
Vintage	**Label**	**YR-10**	**YR-9**	**YR-8**	**YR-7**	**YR-6**	**YR-5**	**YR-4**	**YR-3**	**YR-2**	**YR-1**
1977	Bordeaux	10 / 12	9.5 / 12	9 / 11.5	10 / 14	11 / 15	11 / 13	10 / 12	8 / 12	9 / 12	9 / 12
1919	German Riesling	30 / 40	30 / 40	33 / 40	33 / 43	30 / 38	30 / 35	28 / 37	28 / 40	25 / 35	23 / 30
1990	Napa Cabernet	3 / 4	3 / 4	3.5 / 4.5	3.5 / 4.5	4 / 6	5 / 7	4 / 7	5 / 8	4.5 / 7	4 / 6
1984	Red Burgundy	20 / 31	20 / 35	21 / 35	20 / 32	24 / 32	28 / 35	30 / 35	30 / 37	27 / 30	23 / 27
1943	Alsace Riesling	30 / 48	35 / 50	32 / 50	38 / 50	32 / 50	28 / 50	30 / 50	34 / 50	35 / 48	31 / 42
1919	Rioja	20 / 24	22 / 26	18 / 28	25 / 30	25 / 28	20 / 25	20 / 25	23 / 30	25 / 30	28 / 35
1885	Y'Quem	30 / 35	30 / 35	30 / 35	30 / 35	30 / 35	30 / 35	35 / 40	35 / 40	35 / 40	30 / 35
1955	Vintage Champagne	12 / 15	12 / 15	13 / 17	11 / 15	10 / 17	14 / 20	18 / 22	19 / 20	20 / 24	22 / 25
1994	Red Burgundy	15 / 18	15 / 17	14 / 16	12 / 15	12 / 15	12 / 15	13 / 17	14 / 17	12 / 15	13 / 15
1990	Bordeaux - Pomerol	5 / 7	8 / 12	8 / 12	10 / 13	7 / 10	9 / 14	9 / 15	12 / 15	12 / 17	13 / 17
1986	Bordeaux - Graves	8 / 10	9 / 12	9 / 13	10 / 12	10 / 13	10 / 15	12 / 15	11 / 14	10 / 13	12 / 15
1982	Bordeaux - Lalande	20 / 24	22 / 25	22 / 26	20 / 24	23 / 28	22 / 25	22 / 25	24 / 28	25 / 29	25 / 30
2015	Cote du Rhone	–	2.5 / 4	2.5 / 3.5	3 / 5	3 / 5	3 / 5	4 / 6	4 / 6	4 / 6	5 / 7
2016	Cote du Rhone	–	–	2.5 / 3.5	3 / 5	3 / 5	3 / 5	4 / 6	4 / 6	4 / 6	5 / 7
2013	Barolo	2 / 2.5	2 / 3	2.5 / 4	3 / 4	3.5 / 4.5	4 / 5	4 / 5	5 / 7	5 / 6	5 / 6
2010	Barolo	2 / 2.5	2 / 3	2.5 / 4	3 / 5	3.5 / 5	4 / 5	4 / 6	5 / 8	5 / 8	5 / 8
2015	Super Tuscan	–	3 / 4	3 / 4	3 / 4	3.5 / 4	3.5 /4	4 / 5	4 / 4.5	4 / 5	4 / 6
2010	Brunello	5 / 6	5 / 7	6 / 8	4 / 8	4 / 10	4 / 12	5 / 12	6 / 12	8 / 12	9 / 12
2015	Chianti Classico	–	.5 / 1	.5 / 1.5	1 / 1.5	1 / 2	1.5 / 2	1 / 1.5	2.5 / 3	3 / 4	3 / 5

Exhibit 17

December Email Exchange Between Alvarez and Kondo, Forwarded to Jacobs

Payton Alvarez

From: Alvarez, Payton <payton.alvarez@wind.nita>
To: Jordan Jacobs <jordan.jacobs@wind.nita>
Subject: FW: Request for Proposal—8 bottle rare wine collection
Date: December 2, YR-1 5:42 PM
Attachment: Coveted Collection RFP Response.pdf

JJ—attached is the proposal I received from Coveted Collections, the swanky private auction house that is perfect for our rare wine collection. I know you are flying out later today but let me know if you have thoughts on this RFP. I think this is the one.
Fly safe!

Payton Alvarez
Chief Distribution Officer
Wine Imports and Distribution Partnership

From: Kondo@CovetedCollections.nita
To: Alvarez, Payton <payton.alvarez@wind.nita>; Jacobs, Jordan <jordan.jacobs@wind.nita>
Subject: RE: Request for Proposal—8 bottle rare wine collection
Date: December 1, YR-1 1:15 PM
Attachment: Coveted Collection RFP Response.pdf

Dear Payton Alvarez:
Please find our response to your request for proposal attached to this email. Please let us know if you have any questions, and we truly hope to serve you in an auction of your priceless wine collection.

Truly Yours,

Kondo Mineaux
Owner and Chief Auction Officer

From: Alvarez, Payton <payton.alvarez@wind.nita>
To: Alvarez, Payton <payton.alvarez@wind.nita>; Jacobs, Jordan <jordan.jacobs@wind.nita>
Subject: Request for Proposal—8 bottle rare wine collection
Date: November 20, YR-1 4:42 PM

Dear recipients:

The Wine Imports and Distribution Partnership is going through a voluntary dissolution to cease all operations. The partnership owns eight bottles of rare and highly valuable wine that we would like to sell by auction as soon as practicable.

We have set aside November 27 from 10am to 4pm for you, your appraiser, and any other consultants to come by and inspect the physical bottles. Please let us know if you require a different day or time, and please contact me by phone if you would like to know more about the wines before that visit.

In your proposal, please specially provide us with an estimated sale price (or range) for each bottle of wine, a detailed explanation of your fees and other expenses, the time we can expect to receive the funds at the conclusion of the auction, and any other details about your auction house or approach to selling this collection that would be useful for our consideration.

If you have any questions, please feel free to contact me.

Thank you.

Payton Alvarez
Chief Distribution Officer
Wine Imports and Distribution Partnership

Exhibit 18

Allen Virtual Auction House Confidential Memo (January 1, YR-0)

ALLEN VIRTUAL
Auction House

January 1, YR-0

CONFIDENTIAL MEMO

From: Riley Allen, CEO

To: File

Re: Details from Wine Auctions Held in December YR-1

Vintage	Wine	Est. Win Bid (in thousands)	Winning Bid	Users at Win	#Bids	Open to Hammer
1955	Vintage Champagne	$22 – $25	$ 27,600.00	64	32	14:44
1982	Bordeaux – Lalande-de Pomerol	$29 – $32	$ 12,900.00	78	14	7:22
1986	Bordeaux – Graves	$12 – $15	$ 14,500.00	91	19	9:37
1990	Bordeaux – Pomerol	$15 – $20	$ 28,400.00	39	40	15:57
			$ 83,400.00			
2003	Vintage Port	$10 –$12	$ 9,100.00	44	25	9:01
2007	Vintage Port	$8 – $10	$ 7,400.00	52	18	5:30
2011	Vintage Port	$4 – $6	$ 3,100.00	51	14	5:12
2015	Cote du Rhone	$4 – $6	$ 7,800.00	28	28	7:58
2016	Cote du Rhone	$4 – $6	$ 8,100.00	25	33	9:40
			$ 35,500.00			
2013	Barolo	$6 – $8	$ 7,700.00	71	55	17:26
2010	Barolo	$6 – $8	$ 9,400.00	77	58	16:49
2015	Super Tuscan	$4 – $6	$ 7,500.00	92	49	14:03
2010	Brunello	$10 – $12	$ 14,100.00	91	62	18:35
2015	Chianti Classico	$4 – $5	$ 7,200.00	46	36	13:54
			$ 45,900.00			
			$ 164,800.00			

Verified by: Riley Allen, CEO Jan. 1, YR-0

Exhibit 19

Allen Virtual Auction House Confidential Memo (November 29, YR-1)

ALLEN VIRTUAL
Auction House

November 29, YR-1

CONFIDENTIAL MEMO

From: Del Murphy, Chief Wine Appraiser

To: Riley Allen, CEO

Re: Appraisal, Inspection, and Review of Wine Collection Owned by the Wine Imports and Distribution Partnership ("the partnership")

Riley—per your request, this memo serves as my final review and opinion regarding the wine collection owned by the partnership for purposes of preparing our response to the partnership's request for proposal. If you have any questions, please do not hesitate to contact me.

Documents and Tangible Things Reviewed

1) Physical inspection and examination of eight bottles of wine on Nov. 27, YR-1
2) Internal analysis and records related to same bottles and recent wine auctions
3) Analysis and review of external research and data related to auction pricing, auction attendance, and ratings and evaluations of rare wine

Summary of Wine Bottle Inspection – Visual

1885 Y'Quem

- Excellent exterior condition given age; label undamaged with slight ink fading
- Minor ullage, less than would be expected for vintage
- No capsule; 0.3 cm cork depression with no signs of seepage, no concern
- Deep golden color consistent with age
- No evidence of fraud or tampering

1919 Rioja

- Moderate-plus exterior condition; slight label tearing; major ink fading
- Moderate-minus ullage, within expectations for vintage
- Capsule in place; cork feels level with no signs of seepage
- Orange and sunset hues from loss of color is consistent with age
- No evidence of fraud or tampering

1919 German Riesling

- Near perfect exterior condition, only minor ink fading as expected
- Medium ullage—within risk tolerance
- No capsule; 0.2 cm cork extension—suggests possible heat exposure, low concern
- No evidence of fraud or tampering or seepage

1943 Alsace Riesling

- Near perfect exterior condition with no discernable ink fading
- Slight ullage suggesting exceptional storage conditions
- No capsule; 0.2 cm cork depression, no signs of seepage; no concern
- No evidence of fraud or tampering

1955 Champagne

- Moderate exterior condition; label damage, ink fading, and peeling
- Cork cage shows no damage or concern
- No evidence of fraud or tampering

1977 Bordeaux

- Moderate exterior condition; front label difficult to read with minor damage
- Moderate-plus ullage, more than expected but still low/moderate concern
- Capsule; cork feels slightly extruded but unconfirmed; no signs of seepage
- No evidence of fraud or tampering

1984 Red Bordeaux

- Excellent exterior condition given age; label undamaged
- Very slight ullage, far less than would be expected for vintage
- Capsule; cork feels level; no signs of seepage
- No evidence of fraud or tampering

1990 Napa Cabernet

- Moderate-plus exterior condition; label undamaged
- No ullage present nor expected
- Capsule; cork feels level; no signs of seepage
- No evidence of fraud or tampering

Market Factors

The market for rare and/or old wine in Nita is relatively sparse, both in terms of buyers and sellers, but the volume and value of wines auctioned in Nita has grown at an average yearly pace of 10 percent or more in the last five years. An anonymous survey of bidders at private auctions in YR-1 revealed that approximately 50 percent of bidders were from outside the State of Nita (mostly California, Texas, and New York). Growing interest from outside the State of Nita is widely believed to be part of the reason for strong market growth. Interest outside of Nita is even stronger for public online auctions of similarly priced wine, which makes sense since buyers do not need to travel to Nita. From our significant investment and research into offering wine auctions, we conclude that approximately 75–100 unique users would attend an online auction for five bottles worth approximately $75,000 to $100,000. I believe that number will grow with each successive wine auction if you apply the same parameters.

Evaluations and Estimates

Evaluations and estimates for rare wine involve both objective and subjective components, and thus it is not atypical for estimates to vary considerably even among respected wine experts such as Parker Roberts, Jancis Robbins, or Juan Dauvy. I have relied largely on the evaluations from Parker Roberts's *Vine Acuity* because those are considered the most accurate on the market and they were recently updated—on October 15, to be precise. I accessed and reviewed that data on November 28, the day after our in-person inspection of the wine.

Auction Order

Our research and experience has taught us that clients—and many auction houses—are poor at picking the most advantageous order for auction items. While there may be marketing or timing benefits to listing certain items first or near the beginning (for one-by-one auctions, of course), the general best practice is to order the wines in descending value. The one exception that may benefit us is to list an average valued wine first as a safety net in case bidders take longer to log in or otherwise are tardy to the start of the auction. Although our minimum floor pricing already addresses some of this risk, we have found this strategy effective.

Recommendations

Based on the information I reviewed and outlined in this memorandum, I believe, with a 95 percent confidence level, the partnership's wine will sell at the following prices (assuming they are auctioned in this order). I have also indicated my recommendation for the minimum floor prices—which, as I've stated many times, cannot be aggressive. If a buyer loses the right to purchase wine because it did not hit the unknown minimum floor, that will be a difficult marketing and messaging campaign that could severely damage our entry into this new business market.

1)	1943 Alsace Riesling	$38,500	($20,000 floor)
2)	1885 Y'Quem	$32,250	($17,500 floor)
3)	1919 Rioja	$33,800	($17,500 floor)
4)	1984 Red Burgundy	$23,150	($15,000 floor)
5)	1919 German Riesling	$27,200	($15,000 floor)
6)	1995 Vintage Champagne	$22,400	($10,000 floor)
7)	1977 Bordeaux	$ 9,900	($ 4,000 floor)
8)	1990 Napa Cabernet	$ 5,700	($ 2,500 floor)

Based on our prior financial analysis of pricing fees for customers selling high-value wine, I recommend offering our standard terms (higher of $2,500/per or 15 percent of sale) and then retreating to our fallback offer when they negotiate ($1,000/per + 5 percent).

Assuming the fallback terms and my estimates above, that would generate approximately $17,500 in fees for AVAH. I would not recommend spending any more than $7,500 on advertising, promotions, etc. because this will eat substantially into our margins, but I understand risking margins on our first auction could pay sizeable dividends in the future.

Printed, reviewed, and confirmed on Nov. 29, YR-1; hand delivered to Riley at 2:30pm

Del Murphy

Exhibit 20

Vine Acuity Blog Page, September 5, YR-11

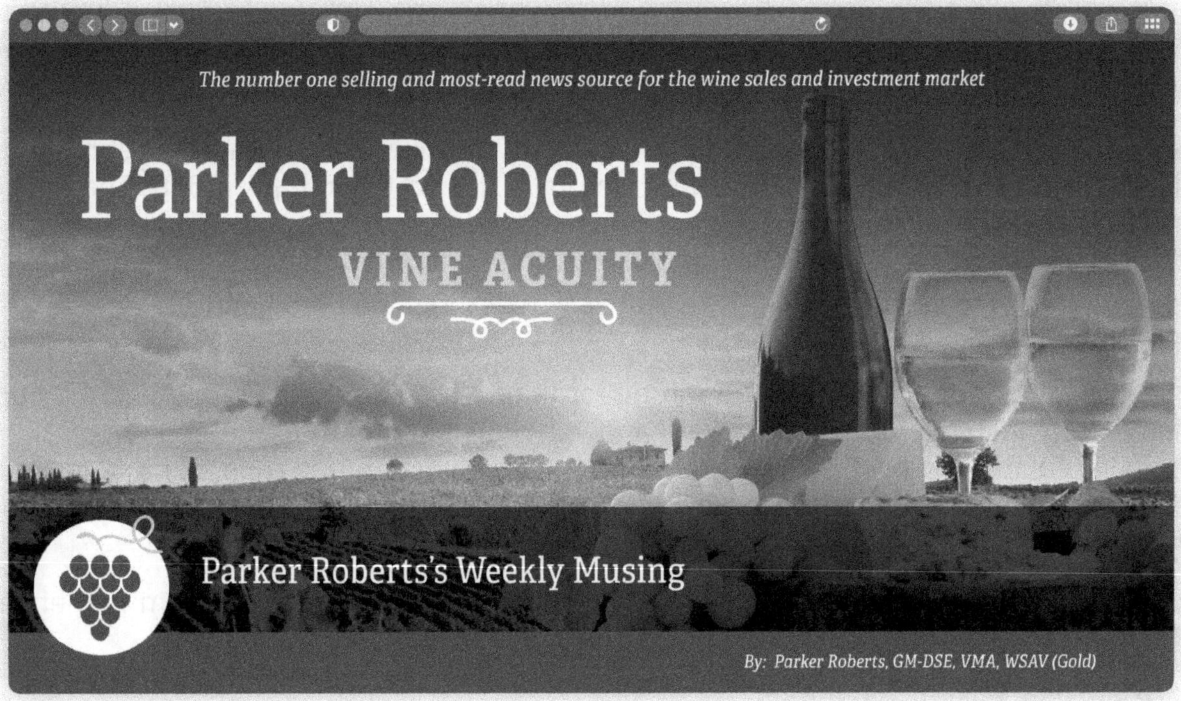

September 5, YR-11

"The United States of America." We've grown accustomed to hearing the USA top the list in international competitions. There are exceptions, of course. Olympic doubles ping pong. That ski race competition where they shoot at those tiny targets. I'm generally OK with that. Can't win them all.

That usually applies to wine, too. No offense to the fabulous wines grown in Napa, Sonoma, Willamette, Finger Lakes, and the other fantastic regions in this great country. But France, Italy, and the like are the originals. And not just making wine; tasting wine as well. The job of tasting wine goes back centuries in those countries, a tradition designed to establish quality levels and pricing—a tradition that stills exist today in nearly the same form. (See History of Growths in Bordeaux.)

Until a few weeks ago, you would have been forgiven for assuming those countries deserved the same deference for competitive blind wine tasting. Until a few weeks ago, you would have been justified—but I am getting ahead of myself.

There are a variety of formats for blind tasting, but the World Wine Tasting Match is considered the gold standard for international events: two-person teams, twelve wines, and seventy-five minutes to submit one scoresheet per team. Points are awarded for correctly identifying the sole or majority grape, country and region of origin, and the vintage. The team element is the most unique, and it has led to several eventful moments in the past (see Monaco Fights Mid-Match).

This year's competition was held at the grand Palais Chambord in the Loire Valley, France. Thirty-nine countries sent teams to the competition, and the results were revealed in the traditional method of reading the top ten finishers from ten to one. (The entire rankings are later released and can be found here.)

Payton Alvarez and Jordan Jacobs, a rag-tag duo of a banker and sommelier, represented the USA after a surprising and dominant victory at the US Open back in July. The host of the US Open later characterized them as the most balanced and complementary team of blind tasters he'd ever seen. And, boy, was he right. I only wish I had been there in Chambord to see the open-mouthed shock on the rest of the field, especially those countries who have bad-mouthed our performance in the past (receipts kept here, here, and here).

True congratulations to Payton and Jordan for their remarkable accomplishment. I hope their victory inspires more sommeliers and wine aficionados to practice and partake in the skill of blind tasting. Even if you are not entering any competitions, blind tasting will teach you indispensable lessons about your personal taste and how to identify quality and value.

I look forward to seeing what comes next for Payton and Jordan. And I am immensely proud of their victory.

Here's to you, Payton and Jordan!

Parker

Select Law, Jury Instructions, and Verdict Form

Select Law from Nita Uniform Partnership Code

Section 101. Title.

This statute shall be titled the "Nita Uniform Partnership Code" and may be abbreviated and referenced as the "Nita UPC" in all court filings and submissions.

Section 105. Partnership Agreement; Scope, Function, and Limitations.

(a) Except as otherwise provided in subsections (c) and (d), the partnership agreement governs:

(1) relations among the partners as partners and between the partners and the partnership;

(2) the business of the partnership and the conduct of that business; and,

(3) the means and conditions for amending the partnership agreement.

(b) To the extent the partnership agreement does not provide for a matter described in subsection (a), this Nita UPC governs the matter.

(c) A partnership agreement may not:

(1) alter or eliminate the duty of loyalty or the duty of care, except as otherwise provided in subsection (d);

(2) relieve or exonerate a person from liability for conduct involving bad faith, willful or intentional misconduct, or knowing violation of law;

(3) vary the causes of dissolution specified in Section 801(b) or (c);

(4) vary the requirement to wind up the partnership's business as specified in Section 802(a), (b)(1), and (c);

(d) Without limiting other terms that may be included in a partnership agreement, the following rules apply:

(1) To the extent the partnership agreement expressly relieves a partner of a responsibility that the partner would otherwise have under this Nita UPC and imposes the responsibility on one or more other partners, the agreement also may eliminate or limit any fiduciary duty of the partner relieved of the responsibility which would have pertained to the responsibility.

(2) If not manifestly unreasonable, the partnership agreement may:

(A) identify specific types or categories of activities that do not violate the duty of loyalty;

(B) alter the duty of care, but may not authorize conduct involving bad faith, willful or intentional misconduct, or knowing violation of law; and

(C) alter or eliminate any other fiduciary duty.

(e) The court shall decide as a matter of law whether a term of a partnership agreement is manifestly unreasonable under subsection (d)(2). The court:

(1) shall make its determination as of the time the challenged term became part of the partnership agreement and by considering only circumstances existing at that time; and

(2) may invalidate the term only if, in light of the purposes and business of the partnership, it is readily apparent that:

(A) the objective of the term is unreasonable; or

(B) the term is an unreasonable means to achieve the term's objective.

(f) A jury shall decide as a question of fact whether any actions or decisions by a partner related to liquidation, dissolution, or winding up the partnership were in the best interest of an orderly dissolution as described in Section 806.

Section 401. Partner's Rights.

(a) Each partner is entitled to an equal share of the partnership distributions and, except in the case of a limited liability partnership, is chargeable with a share of the partnership losses in proportion to the partner's share of the distributions.

(b) Each partner has equal rights in the management and conduct of the partnership's business.

(c) A partner may use or possess partnership property only on behalf of the partnership.

(d) A partner is not entitled to remuneration for services performed for the partnership, except for reasonable compensation for services rendered in winding up the business of the partnership.

Section 402. Partner's Duties.

Partners owe the following fiduciary duties to each other and the partnership:

(a) Duty of loyalty and duty of care;

(b) Duty of the utmost good faith, fairness, and honesty in dealings with each other on matters pertaining to the partnership;

(c) Duty to refrain from self-dealing and from competition with the partnership, which extends to dealings with a fiduciary's spouse, agents, employees, and other persons whose interests are closely identified with those of the fiduciary; and,

(d) Duty to fully disclose all matters affecting the partnership, which includes all important information concerning any transaction, including any matters that might influence a fiduciary to act in a manner prejudicial to the partnership.

Section 801. Events Causing Dissolution.

A partnership is dissolved, and its business must be wound up, upon the occurrence of any of the following:

(a) an event or circumstance that the partnership agreement states causes dissolution;

(b) on application by a partner, the entry by the appropriate court of an order dissolving the partnership on the grounds that:

(1) the conduct of all or substantially all the partnership's business is unlawful;

(2) the economic purpose of the partnership is likely to be unreasonably frustrated;

(3) another partner has engaged in conduct relating to the partnership business which makes it not reasonably practicable to carry on the business in partnership with that partner; or

(4) it is otherwise not reasonably practicable to carry on the partnership business in conformity with the partnership agreement;

(c) by consent of all partners in the partnership; or

(d) the passage of ninety consecutive days during which the partnership does not have at least two partners.

Section 802. Winding Up.

(a) A dissolved partnership shall wind up its business, and the partnership continues after dissolution only for the purpose of winding up.

(b) In winding up its business, the partnership:

(1) shall discharge the partnership's debts, obligations, and other liabilities, settle and close the partnership's business, and marshal and distribute the assets of the partnership; and

(2) may:

(A) deliver to the Nita Secretary of State for filing a statement of dissolution stating the name of the partnership and that the partnership is dissolved;

(B) preserve the partnership business and property as a going concern for a reasonable time;

(C) prosecute and defend actions and proceedings, whether civil, criminal, or administrative;

(D) transfer the partnership's property;

(E) settle disputes by mediation or arbitration;

(F) deliver to the Nita Secretary of State for filing a statement of termination stating the name of the partnership and that the partnership is terminated; and

(G) perform other acts necessary or appropriate to the winding up.

(c) On the application of any partner, the appropriate court may order judicial supervision of the winding up of a dissolved partnership, including the appointment of a person to wind up the partnership's business, if:

(1) the partnership does not have a partner and within a reasonable time following the dissolution no person has been appointed; or,

(2) the applicant establishes other good cause.

Section 806. Best Interest of an Orderly Dissolution.

When selling an asset during dissolution, a partner's decision as to the details of the sale must be in the best interest of an orderly dissolution. Whether or not a chosen liquidation method is in the best interest of an orderly dissolution is a question of fact governed by the following factors—none of which alone is dispositive:

(1) **Amount of expected cash proceeds**—including consideration of the gross revenue, amount of fees and expenses compared to net proceeds;

(2) **Receipt of net proceeds**—including how soon after the sale the net proceeds are received free and clear of any liabilities related to the liquidated assets; and

(3) **Unique market conditions**—including the abundance or scarcity of similar assets for sale, and the abundance or scarcity of potential buyers for similar assets.

Where the price of the asset is unknown prior to deciding on a sale method—such as when deciding between a public and private auction—a partner may rely on estimates, appraisals, or other forward-looking analysis when choosing one sale method over the other and still meet the "best interest of an orderly dissolution" standard provided the partner performs a reasonable amount of thorough diligence into the information relied upon.

Section 807. Consequences of Decisions Not in the Best Interest of an Orderly Liquidation.

If a partner unilaterally chooses a sale method that is not in the best interest of an orderly liquidation of the partnership, then that partner shall bear personal liability for any damages resulting from that decision.

Section 901. Statute of Limitations.

Unless all partners agree in writing to the contrary, a partner's right to sue any other partner in relation to the partnership terminates upon the filing of a notice of dissolution or termination of the partnership with the Nita Secretary of State.

Jury Instructions

Introduction

You have been selected as jurors and have taken an oath to well and truly decide this cause. This trial will last one day. During the progress of the trial, there will be times when the court recesses or otherwise excuses the jurors from the courtroom. During those periods of time, you must not talk about this case among yourselves or with anyone else.

During the trial, do not talk to the parties, their lawyers, or any of the witnesses. If any attempt is made by anyone to talk to you concerning the matters here under consideration, you should immediately report that fact to the court through the bailiff.

You should keep an open mind throughout this trial. You should not form or express any opinion, verbally or nonverbally, during the trial and should reach no conclusion in this case until you have heard all the evidence, the arguments of counsel, and the final instructions as to the law that will be given to you by the court.

Conduct of the Trial

First, the attorneys will have an opportunity to make opening statements. These statements are not evidence and should be considered only as a preview of what the attorneys expect the evidence will be.

Following the opening statements, witnesses will be called to testify. They will be placed under oath and questioned by the attorneys. Documents and other tangible exhibits may also be received as evidence. If an exhibit is given to you to examine during the trial, you should examine it carefully, individually, and without comment.

It is the attorneys' right and duty to object when testimony or other evidence is being offered that they believe is not admissible. When the court sustains an objection to a question, you must disregard the question and the answer, if one has been given, and draw no inference from the question or answer or speculate what the witness would have said if permitted to answer. Jurors must also disregard evidence that is stricken from the record.

When the evidence is completed, the attorneys will make closing arguments. These closing arguments are not evidence but are given to assist you in evaluating the evidence. The attorneys are permitted to argue in an attempt to persuade you to a particular verdict. You may accept or reject these closing arguments as you see fit.

Finally, just before you retire to consider your verdict, I will give you further instructions on how the law applies to this case.

Final Instructions

Members of the jury, the evidence in this case has been completed, and I will now instruct you as to the law.

The law applicable to this case is stated in these instructions and it is your duty and obligation to follow all of them in reaching your verdict. You must not single out certain instructions and disregard others, but rather you must follow all the applicable law I will give you.

It is your duty to determine the facts and to determine them only from the evidence in this case. You are to apply the law to the facts and in this way decide the case. You must not be governed or influenced by sympathy or prejudice for or against any party in this case. Your verdict must be based on the evidence and not upon speculation, guess, conjecture, or emotion.

From time to time, the court has ruled on the admissibility of evidence. You must not concern yourselves with the reasons for those rulings. You should disregard questions and exhibits that were withdrawn or to which objections were sustained. You should also disregard testimony and exhibits that the court has refused or stricken.

The evidence that you should consider consists only of the witnesses' testimonies and the exhibits the court has received. Any evidence that was received for a limited purpose should not be considered by you for any other purpose. You should consider all the evidence in the light of your own observations and experiences in life.

Neither by these instructions nor by any rulings or remarks that I have made do I mean to indicate any opinion about the facts or what your verdict should be.

You are the sole judges of the credibility of the witnesses and of the weight to be given, if any, to the testimony of each witness. In determining what credit to give any witness, you may take into account the witness's ability and opportunity to observe the matters testified to; their manner and appearance while testifying; any bias, interest, or prejudice the witness may have; the reasonableness of the testimony considered in light of all the evidence; and any other factors that bear on the believability and weight of the witness's testimony.

You have heard evidence in this case from witnesses who testified as experts. The law allows experts to express an opinion on subjects involving their specialized knowledge, training and skill, experience, or research. While they were allowed to give their opinions, it is entirely within the province of the jury to determine what weight to give their testimony. Jurors are not bound by the testimony of experts; weigh their testimony as you would that of any other witness.

The law recognizes two kinds of evidence—direct and circumstantial. Direct evidence proves a fact directly; that is, the evidence itself, if true, establishes the fact. Circumstantial evidence is the proof of facts or circumstances that given rise to a reasonable inference of other facts; that is, circumstantial evidence proves a fact indirectly in that it follows from other facts or circumstances according to common experience and observations in life. An eyewitness is a common example of direct evidence, while human footprints are circumstantial evidence that a person was present.

The law makes no distinction between direct and circumstantial evidence as to the degree or amount of proof required, and each should be considered according to whatever weight or value it may have. Consider and evaluate all the evidence in arriving at your verdict.

The court will now instruct you about the claims and defenses of each party to the case and the law governing the case. Please pay close attention to these instructions. You must arrive at your verdict by applying the law as you are now instructed to the facts as you find them to be.

The parties in this case are Jordan Jacobs, the plaintiff, and Payton Alvarez, the defendant. The parties have agreed to, and you must regard as conclusively proven, the following facts:

a) The settlement agreement is a valid and enforceable contract;

b) The wine sold by Coveted Collections on December 7, YR-1, cannot be returned to the partnership; and,

c) Burgundian law provides that individual owners of an entity that has terminated or dissolved are personally liable for any claims a French citizen may have against the entity.

The burden of proof is on the plaintiff to prove the defendant breached the settlement agreement by a preponderance of the evidence. "Preponderance of the evidence" means the greater weight and degree of credible evidence admitted in this case.

For the plaintiff to prevail on its claim for breach of contract, you must find the following proposition has been proved:

a) The defendant's decision to sell the partnership's wine collection with Coveted Collections breached the settlement agreement because that decision was not in the best interests of an orderly dissolution.

Whether the choice to sell the wine was in the "best interests of an orderly dissolution" is a subjective test. The law provides three factors—none of which are more important than the other—to guide you in your decision. First, the expected cash proceeds from the sale, including the amount of fees and expenses compared to the net proceeds. Second, the speed by which the partnership received the net proceeds without any further liability related to the wine sold. Third, whether there are any unique market conditions for the sale of rare wine, including how many or few similar assets are for sale, and how many or few potential buyers there are.

If you find that the proposition has not been proved by a preponderance of the evidence, then your verdict must be for the defendant.

If you find that the proposition has been proved by a preponderance of the evidence, then your verdict must be for the plaintiff—*unless*

a) the defendant proves one of their affirmative defenses by a preponderance of the evidence.

The defendant has raised two defenses to the plaintiff's breach of contract claim: 1) consent; and 2) ratification.

For the plaintiff to have *consented* to the defendant's decision to engage Coveted Collections, the defendant must prove by a preponderance of the evidence that the plaintiff approved the decision consistent with the requirements of the partnership agreement. That means there is a separate writing that contains the defendant's proposal with reasonable specificity and the plaintiff's consent, approval, or agreement to that proposal.

To prove the plaintiff *ratified* the defendant's decision to engage Coveted Collections, the defendant must prove by a preponderance of the evidence that the plaintiff, after learning all the material facts about the private auction with Coveted Collections, approved the decision by acts, words, or conduct. Ratification may be either express or implied. Express ratification is typically where the plaintiff agrees in writing to confirm or accept the earlier act. Implied ratification can be established where the plaintiff's words or actions clearly evidence an intent to ratify the decision. Implied ratification does not have to be shown by express word or deed and may be inferred by a party's course of conduct.

Because this is a bifurcated trial, you will not decide the amount of damages, if any, if you find either or both parties are liable to the other. If it is necessary to determine any amount of damages at the conclusion of this trial, a separate trial will be held to make that determination.

You must not be concerned with the wisdom of any rule of law. Regardless of any opinions you may have as to what the law ought to be, it would be a violation of your sworn duty to base a verdict upon any other view of the law than that given in the instructions of this court.

IN THE SUPERIOR COURT
IN AND FOR THE COUNTY OF DARROW
AND STATE OF NITA

JORDAN JACOBS Plaintiff, v. PAYTON ALVAREZ Defendant.	§ § § § § § §	Civil Action No. 95-1984

VERDICT FORM

The following questions will be presented for the jury's unanimous decision.

Please answer the following question "YES" or "NO." Do you find by a preponderance of the credible evidence that:

1. **Payton Alvarez breached the settlement agreement by selling the partnership's wine collection with Coveted Collections?**

YES _______

NO _______

If you answered NO to Question 1, then you are finished—please sign and return this verdict for this to the bailiff.

If you answered YES to Question 1, then you must answer the following question:

Please answer the following question "YES" or "NO." Do you find by a preponderance of the credible evidence that:

2. **Jordan Jacobs gave consent for Payton Alvarez to sell the partnership's wine collection with Coveted Collections?**

YES _______

NO _______

If you answered YES to Question 2, then you are finished—please sign and return this verdict for this to the bailiff.

If you answered NO to Question 2, then you must answer the following question:

Please answer the following question "YES" or "NO." Do you find by a preponderance of the credible evidence that:

3. **Jordan Jacobs ratified Payton Alvarez's decision to sell the partnership's wine collection with Coveted Collections?**

YES _______

NO _______

FOREPERSON: Sign and return this verdict form to the court's bailiff.

______________________ ___________

Foreperson Date

APPENDICES

Special Impeachment Problems

Problem 1: Jordan Jacobs

Assume that Jordan Jacobs has testified at trial on direct examination that they don't need the money they are seeking from this lawsuit, and that they are suing Alvarez purely on principle.

(a) For Alvarez, conduct a cross-examination and impeachment of Jordan Jacobs.

(b) For Jacobs, conduct a redirect examination to the extent necessary to rehabilitate.

Problem 2: Jordan Jacobs

Assume that Jordan Jacobs has testified at trial on direct examination that their flight to France in December YR-1 cost the same as every other international flight taken on behalf of the partnership.

(c) For Alvarez, conduct a cross-examination and impeachment of Jordan Jacobs.

(d) For Jacobs, conduct a redirect examination to the extent necessary to rehabilitate.

Problem 3: Payton Alvarez

Assume that Payton Alvarez has testified at trial on direct examination that they attended the auction at Coveted Collections. Assume further that Alvarez testified on direct examination: "I was not disappointed with the final sale price of any of our wines sold at the auction."

(a) For Jacobs, conduct a cross-examination and impeachment of Payton Alvarez.

(b) For Alvarez, conduct a redirect examination to the extent necessary to rehabilitate.

Problem 4: Payton Alvarez

Assume that Payton Alvarez has testified at trial on direct examination that the only auction that would have been in the "best interest of an orderly dissolution" was the auction hosted by Coveted Collections.

(c) For Jacobs, conduct a cross-examination and impeachment of Payton Alvarez.

(d) For Alvarez, conduct a redirect examination to the extent necessary to rehabilitate.

Problem 5: Riley Allen

Assume that Riley Allen has testified at trial on direct examination that, when asked to compare the payment terms between AVAH and Coveted Collections, AVAH pays its customers within the same timeframe as Coveted Collections.

(a) For Alvarez, conduct a cross-examination and impeachment of Riley Allen.

(b) For Jacobs, conduct a redirect examination to the extent necessary to rehabilitate.

Problem 6: Kondo Mineaux

Assume that Kondo Mineaux has testified at trial on direct examination that every bidder who was invited to attend the auction of the partnership's wine collection showed up at the auction.

(a) For Jacobs, conduct a cross-examination and impeachment of Kondo Mineaux.

(b) For Alvarez, conduct a redirect examination to the extent necessary to rehabilitate.

Problem 7: Courtney "Corky" Gardner

Assume that Courtney "Corky" Gardner has testified at trial on direct examination that they told Mineaux that it was unethical for Mineaux's brother-in-law to be bidding at a Coveted Collections auction. Assume further that Gardner's trip to Europe was, in fact, cancelled, and thus Gardner was able to attend trial.

(a) For Alvarez, conduct a cross-examination and impeachment of Courtney "Corky" Gardner.

(b) For Jacobs, conduct a redirect examination to the extent necessary to rehabilitate.

Special Exhibit Problems

Exhibit Problem 1

Assume that Del Murphy passed away on November 28, YR-1 before creating Exhibit 19, and that Allen found three pages of handwritten notes regarding the partnerships' wine collection in Murphy's office the next day. Allen relied on the notes to create Exhibit 6 and then stored the notes in an unlocked file cabinet, which was accessible to any of the five employees who work in AVAH's office. After giving their deposition—but prior to trial—Allen was deposed by Alvarez's attorneys. Allen brought the handwritten notes to the deposition, which are in pencil and have several signs of erasures, and testifies that the notes are in Murphy's handwriting. Allen further testifies that they did not write or erase anything on the notes. After the deposition, the parties agree to send the notes to an expert in handwriting analysis who is unable to conclude with a reasonable degree of scientific certainty that the notes were written by Murphy—but the expert does opine the notes are more likely than not in Murphy's handwriting. Assume the expert is testifying at trial.

(a) For Jacobs, offer the handwritten notes and expert report into evidence.

(b) For Alvarez, oppose the offer.

Exhibit Problem 2

Assume that Courtney "Corky" Gardner did not resell the 1955 Champagne with AVAH because they discovered that the bottle was a forgery. Gardner complained to Coveted Collections and insisted on a refund, but Coveted Collections denied the bottle was a forgery. Gardner filed a lawsuit against Coveted Collections for breach of contract based on the terms and conditions of the auction, which guaranteed the authenticity of all wines auctioned.

(a) Assume Gardner testifies that they stored the Champagne bottle in a locked wine cellar immediately after taking possession and kept it there until trial.

    For Gardner, lay a foundation and offer the Champagne bottle into evidence.

    For Coveted Collections, oppose the offer.

(b) Assume instead that the 1955 Champagne bottle was destroyed when it was tested by an expert in wine forgery prior to trial.

    For Gardner, lay a foundation and offer a Champagne bottle that is like the 1955 Champagne into evidence.

    For Coveted Collections, oppose the offer.

Exhibit Problem 3

Assume that Exhibit 9 has been admitted into evidence pre-trial. For Jacobs, identify two issues or facts that you would like to prove that involve the "Final Auction Invoice" or the "Automated Bid Tracking Log" in Exhibit 9. Use Exhibit 6 or 19 to assist you in proving those two issues. Lay a foundation and offer the exhibit. If admissibility is achieved, use the exhibit with Exhibit 9 in some manner that helps your case. For Alvarez, identify two issues or facts that you would like to prove that involve the "Final Auction Invoice" or the "Automated Bid Tracking Log" in Exhibit 9. Use Exhibit 8 to assist you in proving those two issues. Lay a foundation and offer the exhibit. If admissibility is achieved, use the exhibit with Exhibit 9 in some manner that helps your case.

Exhibit Problem 4

Assume that Exhibit 14 was created by a software program that uses artificial intelligence and algorithms to analyze data linked to an employee's calendar, corporate credit card, and receipts related to travel. The expense report in Exhibit 14 was generated by the software program for Jacobs's trip to France from December 3 to December 10, YR-1. The partners have stipulated to the dollar amounts in Exhibit 14 are correct based on bank records, but they have lost access to their company email, calendar, and accounting records. Assume further that Jacobs will testify that the entries and information in Exhibit 14 are accurate to the best of their knowledge, and that Alvarez has previously testified in a deposition that they never found any errors in any of the six expense reports created by the software program prior to Exhibit 14.

(a) For Jacobs, lay a foundation and offer Exhibit 14 into evidence.

(b) For Alvarez, develop all possible objections to the admissibility of Exhibit 14.

Exhibit Problem 5

Assume that Parker Roberts is available to testify at trial and that Roberts personally prepared and created all of the data and information reflected in Exhibit 16. For Jacobs and Alvarez, identify one or more wines on Exhibit 16 to question Roberts about on direct examination. Pay particular attention to ensuring your questions are clear if referring to specific numbers or cells on the table.

(a) Lay a business records foundation for the admission of Exhibit 16 into evidence. The opposing party will object to any deficiency in the business records foundation.

(b) If admissibility is achieved, seek permission from the court to have Roberts step down from the witness chair for demonstrative purpose.

(c) If permission is granted, examine Roberts about Exhibit 16 in a demonstrative manner.

www.ingramcontent.com/pod-product-compliance
Lightning Source LLC
LaVergne TN
LVHW082351200926
848481LV00012B/3536